Information System Specification and Design Road Map

Information System Specification and Design Road Map

DENIS CONNOR

Prentice-Hall, Inc., Englewood Cliffs, New Jersey 07632

Library of Congress Cataloging in Publication Data

Connor, Denis (date)
    Information system specification and design
road map.

    Includes bibliographies and index.
    1. Management information systems—Design and
construction. I. Title.
T58.6.C668 1985   658.4'038   84-24979
ISBN 0-13-464868-4

Editorial/production supervision
  and interior design: Diana Drew
Cover design: Ben Santora
Manufacturing buyer: Gordon Osbourne

Printed in the United States of America

10 9 8 7 6 5 4 3 2 1

ISBN 0-13-464868-4 01

Prentice-Hall International, Inc., *London*
Prentice-Hall of Australia Pty. Limited, *Sydney*
Editora Prentice-Hall do Brasil, Ltda., *Rio de Janeiro*
Prentice-Hall Canada Inc., *Toronto*
Prentice-Hall Hispanoamericana, S.A., *Mexico*
Prentice-Hall of India Private Limited, *New Delhi*
Prentice-Hall of Japan, Inc., *Tokyo*
Prentice-Hall of Southeast Asia Pte. Ltd., *Singapore*
Whitehall Books Limited, *Wellington, New Zealand*

59,972

To Connie
and all our family,
with love

Contents

Foreword

The need for a radically different approach to the development of large information processing systems became apparent in the late 1960s and early 1970s. With this need came an evaluation of existing design practices and the realization that those practices were inadequate. Several new software design methods were introduced with some methods indirectly suggesting an engineering design approach. Other methods claimed to be engineering approaches, but were so in name only. One paper referred to software engineering as a branch of mathematics. After a considerable amount of research and careful evaluation of the material related to software development methods in general, and software engineering in particular, it became apparent that there was no published, uniform treatment of this subject. In the frantic scramble to find ways to improve the production of reliable and cost-effective software, industry has essentially approached software engineering much like the proverbial group of blind men and their various interpretations of the physical characteristics of the elephant.

Computer professionals began to preach the gospel of top-down design, structured coding, and software life-cycle management. Concepts like "modular design" and "structured programming" became buzzwords for the new technology. Yet, as we watch what the average software development organization does, as compared to what it says it does, it is apparent that the process of designing software systems is still an art (or craft) characterized by considerable folklore, black magic, and bursts of inspiration. The introduction of one or more of the "modern" specification and design approaches has met with dismal failure in many instances because the goals and proper use of the method was not fully understood. Techniques are often misapplied due to either a misconception that a single method is best suited for all applications, or fear of change makes the selection of an approach determined by the application from multiple approaches unacceptable.

Connor's book is the first successful attempt at removing the mist (or should I say fog) that surrounds the application of the major system specification and design approaches to software development. The text provides a clear, concise, and logical description of each of the development approaches and the way the specific method fits into the software development cycle. The presentation appears essentially independent of the reader's focus, whether it be management, analysis, design, or coding.

One of the most rewarding features of the text is the uniform and objective treatment given to each of the specification and design methods. The presentation makes it possible to understand the application of each method to software development through the use of a "road map." This understanding can be gained without reference to any of the alternate methods described in the text, much like an encyclopedia. The material can also be used to compare the implementation of alternate development methods in the software life cycle by essentially comparing the associated road maps. Since Connor has no particular method to sell, the presentation is free of the sales pitch that typically accompanies specific specification and design method texts. The supporting bibliography allows the reader to pursue more detailed and specific texts on each of the individual methods.

The text encompasses a broad set of specification and design approaches. The list of approaches includes

- *Information Engineering*, introduced by Clive Finkelstein and James Martin.
- *Structured Analysis and Design*, a la Yourdon, Constantine, De Marco, Gane and Sarzen, and Meyers.
- *Structured Requirements Definition*, supported by Ken Orr.
- *Jackson System Development*, developed by Michael Jackson.
- *Higher Order Software*, as supported by James Martin.
- *Prototyping*

Of course, there is more to mastering a development method or technique than reading a text, even one as well written as this is. Connor has assembled an excellent exposition on the "best ways to skin a cat (simplified)," but in the words of Publilius Syrus (42 B.C.), one of my favorite philosophers:

Practice is the best of all instructors.

Randall W. Jensen
Chief Scientist
Software Engineering Division
Ground Systems Group
Hughes Aircraft Company

Preface

This book describes and compares the six best known approaches to information system specification and design. The six approaches are:

1. Data-base-oriented design illustrated using James Martin and Clive Finkelstein's information engineering
2. Structured analysis and design illustrated using Tom DeMarco's, Ed Yourdon's, and Larry Constantine's techniques
3. Output-oriented structured analysis and design as described by Ken Orr
4. Real-world modeling as described by Michael Jackson
5. Prototyping
6. Error-free program design software illustrated using higher-order software developed by Margaret Hamilton and Saydean Zeldin and described by James Martin

This is done by first defining a simple case-study application and then applying each design technique to the case study. Each step in each technique is illustrated with detailed examples so that the reader has a clear understanding of the approach. Where similarities in techniques occur, these are pointed out to the reader. At the conclusion of the discussion of each technique, its advantages and disadvantages are described. No prior knowledge of any of the techniques is needed. The language used is plain English and where technical terms are used, they are defined.

Project management of the system development process is often achieved using project management systems, which are also referred to as application system development methodologies or a similar term. These specialized products are sold by vendors or are developed in-house. Chapter 10 defines the objectives to be met by these project management systems and analyzes in depth the impact of each technique on a generalized model of a project management system.

This text is intended to meet the needs of several audiences. For example, a systems manager could use it to decide which technique is most suitable to develop a particular system; a college or university professor could use it to teach the subject of information system design, to teach comparative system design techniques, or to teach logical data-base design and its impact on system design; a system designer could use it as a detailed reference for the step-by-step process to be followed during the system specification and design process; an end user (a system user outside the systems department) could use it to gain an effective understanding of the system development process and could use it to develop systems or to knowledgeably discuss the system development process to be followed by the systems department; the owner of a microcomputer could use it to design and build systems; and the systems manager could use it to evaluate a project management system.

The book can be divided into three sections: Chapters 1 through 3 introduce the reader to information systems and their design and describe the case study, Chapters 4 through 9 discuss the six different development techniques, and Chapters 10 through 12 round off the subject with discussion of project management, physical data-base design requirements, and combining development techniques. Because each technique is described independent of the others, the reader can either study them all or can pick and choose among them.

The examples used are easy to follow. The case study in particular was designed so that any reader could relate to it. This was done so that the reader could concentrate on the technique or principle being described and not have to spend time and effort understanding the logic in the example processes. Because the examples are simple, the reader should not conclude that these techniques can be applied only in small or simple systems. Every one of these techniques has been applied successfully by organizations around the world to build large and complex systems.

Denis Connor

Acknowledgments

Three people to whom I owe considerable thanks for their advice on improving the content of this book are Randall Jensen, Thomas R. Gildersleeve, and Ian Peaks. Ian, in particular, served as my "devil's advocate" and on several occasions made me rethink and rewrite various topics.

This book was written during a six-month leave of absence from my job at the Worker's Compensation Board, Ontario. I owe a special debt of gratitude to my wife, Connie, and our children for their support during this time, which enabled me to put aside all other considerations and concentrate on the book alone.

Last, but not least, I thank Karl Karlstrom, my acquisitions editor at Prentice-Hall, Inc., for his encouragement and his faith in my abilities, which, to a great extent, gave me the courage to take the time off to write the book.

1

Introduction

1.1 THE NEED FOR A "ROAD MAP" OF INFORMATION SYSTEM SPECIFICATION AND DESIGN

The term *information system* is generally understood to imply a system that provides management with decision-making information. This interpretation is restrictive, as it excludes other types of information, such as *operating information* (the information used by the workers to carry on the business) and *control information* (the information that provides the audit trails). Lately another distinction has been drawn—between management information summarized from historical data and data manipulated through a series of "what if"-type algorithms. The latter are now termed *decision support systems.* In this book we define all systems that produce any form of human-readable data as information systems.

If the science of information system specification and design were to be compared to a large country, it should be taken for granted that visitors could obtain and use a road map which would enable them to plot a route across the country by road and by following this route, reach their destination. Most sciences, such as engineering, medicine, law, architecture, mathematics, physics, and chemistry, have such road maps, and students of these sciences have them at hand to study and to follow. It is truly unfortunate that the science of information system specification, design, and development has no such road map. As a result, there is no consistency in the related computer science subjects taught in universities, and even less consistency in the application of this science in business and industry.

What is generally taught in the universities is a combination of operations research, that is, the application of sophisticated mathematical theory applied on the computer, and a plethora of programming languages. Some universities and colleges have started to move into the field of information systems and are teaching subjects such as data modeling, structured systems design and development, and systems project management. These universities and colleges are to be congratulated for recognizing the need for such skills and for attempting to provide them to their students.

In business and industry, vast and complex systems have been built and are continuing to be built. A few have been built well and a few are being built well. The majority are tied together with string and baling wire. The evidence of this is the cost of systems maintenance, which runs five, ten, and even twenty times the original design and development cost.

All these problems exist despite the tremendous number of textbooks written and easily available on a variety of subjects related to information system design. It has often crossed my mind that this vast amount of information is partially the cause of the problem. The university professor, the student, the systems manager, and the systems analyst do not know where to begin and whom to believe because quite often the experts expound theories that contradict one another. In the business and industrial environments, add to this a demanding user community with a backlog of new systems' requirements and an ever-collapsing group of production systems. Can the systems manager and the analyst cope with these problems and at the same time research new techniques and apply them?

1.2 WHAT THE READER CAN EXPECT TO GET FROM THIS BOOK

This book is intended to be a road map to assist those searching for guidance in information system specification and design. Because it is a road map, it discusses a variety of techniques and illustrates them with examples from the same case study. In this way, the readers can evaluate each technique themselves and decide if it will meet their needs. In addition, the use of a single case study enables readers easily to compare one approach with another. The language used in the text is English and not computerese. Where terms are used that mean different things to different authors and to different readers, they are explained in the specific context. The case study is based on a real-life system that was developed using one set of techniques. This system has been reworked in terms of the other techniques described.

The book has been written and organized to be a reference and a guide. In most instances, it will provide the reader with sufficient information to apply the techniques. Those readers who want or need more detailed information should read the texts on which these chapters are based. The techniques described here can be compared to the cities one would pass through en route and the detailed texts and associated training courses to the city maps one would need to explore them. From the viewpoint of universities and colleges, this text should serve as a foundation on which more effective courses in information system specification and design could be built.

One group not mentioned above is the group of end users who design, develop, and implement their own systems outside the conventional systems departments. This text should provide them with sufficient information to design their own systems.

1.3 TYPES OF TECHNIQUES DISCUSSED

This book is about information system specification and design. It is not about the complete system development process. It does not cover feasibility studies, hardware and software selection, programming, testing, and implementation. If the reader would like more information on the development process, it is discussed in depth in *Application Systems Development Methodologies—Solution or Problem?* by Denis Connor, published by Savant.

The system specification and design techniques discussed here reflect a variety of approaches. They were chosen either because they are well known or because they present a viewpoint or a tool which may serve the reader well. They can be described as structured, stepwise refinement, data oriented, output oriented, process driven, and so on. These terms have become part of the language of computerese. They are interpreted by different authors to mean different things. All these techniques, if used properly, should result in good systems. But each of them has its own strengths and weaknesses and these will also be discussed.

The techniques vary in scope. For example, structured analysis and design do not include the physical system and file design, whereas Jackson system development includes the complete specification, design, and development process. This means that, in some instances, the discussion will exceed system specification and logical design. This is necessary to present the particular author's viewpoint completely.

1.4 REQUIREMENTS OF A WELL-DESIGNED BUSINESS SYSTEM

What is a well-designed business system? An information system is *well designed* if, when put into production:

- It satisfies the user's real information requirements.
- It is easy to use and to operate.
- It is easy to maintain (i.e., to correct problems that occur).
- It is easily modified or enhanced.

1.5 OVERVIEW OF EACH TECHNIQUE

1.5.1 Information Engineering

Information engineering was first described in a series of articles by Clive
Finkelstein in *Computerworld* magazine and was later described in *Information Engineering*, a two-volume text by James Martin and Clive Finkelstein, published by Savant. Finkelstein's company, Information Engineering
(Aust) Pty. Ltd., teaches the subject and publishes an Information Engineering Series. The issue titled "Procedure Formation: Specification (and Design)
by Users," authored by Robert M. Rollason and Clive Finkelstein, was also
used as a reference for this text.

Information Engineering derives data requirements from management
objectives, converts the raw data into stable data structures and relationships
in a data model, takes into account data existing in present systems, and
builds processes and procedures from the data model. Information engineering also covers logical and physical data-base design and interfaces with
management techniques such as corporate planning, strategic requirements
planning, and organizational planning. The user plays the key role throughout the specification and design process and yields place to the systems
analyst and programmer only after the design is completed.

Even though Martin and Finkelstein produced *Information Engineering*
as a joint effort, they each approach the problem differently. Where these
differences occur, they are described separately.

The case-study system used in this book was originally designed and
developed using information engineering. During this development, I found a
way to identify the procedures in a system which differed from both the
Martin and Finkelstein approaches and have described this approach in the
text as well.

1.5.2 Structured Analysis and Design

The subject of structured analysis and design, as it relates to the design of
systems and programs using data flow diagrams and structure charts, has
been described at length by a number of authors, including Ed Yourdon and
Larry Constantine, Tom DeMarco, Chris Gane and Trish Sarson, and Glenford Myers. Each textbook takes a slightly different approach, although
basically they teach the same principles. The two texts used as specific references here are *Structured Analysis and System Specification* by Tom
DeMarco and *Structured Design* by Ed Yourdon and Larry Constantine.
Both books are published by Prentice-Hall.

Structured analysis and design are based on a system hierarchy. During
analysis, the system processes are described graphically as black boxes with
inputs and outputs linked in networks. This network is called a *data flow*

diagram. Each black box is shown as a bubble and the inputs and outputs are data flows. The total system is viewed as a single bubble which is exploded into a bubble network and each bubble in the network is again exploded into separate networks until a "primitive" bubble level is reached. These bubbles are described in language which is based on Bohm and Jacopini's basic constructs (i.e., sequence, iteration, and selection). These "primitives" are termed *minispecifications*.

Data flow diagrams are used to record the present physical system, the present logical system, the proposed logical system, and the proposed physical system. The data flow diagrams are supported by a data dictionary and minispecifications. The data flow diagrams, the data dictionary, and the minispecifications are used to develop logical module hierarchies called *structure charts*. The modules are independent and execute specific functions. The logical modules are "packaged" (grouped) into physical nodules which are programmed and comprise the system.

1.5.3 Structured Requirements Definition

Structured Requirements Definition is the title of a book by Ken Orr, published by Ken Orr and Associates. This system design technique was developed by Ken Orr from work done by Jean D. Warnier and himself. *Structured Requirements Definition* was a follow-up on an earlier book by Orr titled *Structured Systems Development*, published by Yourdon Press.

The principle followed by Orr is that system specification and design are derived from output requirements. The primary tool used is the *Warnier-Orr diagram*, which is a series of brackets which can represent system, program, and data hierarchies. A second tool used is the *entity diagram*, which charts information flows (outputs) between entities (organizational or functional units).

Structured requirements definition is divided into two phases. The first phase is the *logical definition* phase. In this phase the application context, the application functions, and the application results are defined. The second phase is the *physical definition* phase. This phase includes the constraints on the system, the alternative physical solutions, the benefits and risks, and the recommended course of action.

1.5.4 Jackson System Development

Jackson system development (JSD) is a technique developed by Michael Jackson and published in a book of the same name by Prentice-Hall. JSD is based on a model of the real world which is reflected in the computer system. The tools used are structure diagrams, structure text, system specification diagrams, and system implementation diagrams.

The *structure diagrams* represent hierarchies of actions. The actions are associated with entities. These are defined using the *structure text*. The *system specification diagrams* and the *system implementation diagrams* use a special Jackson notation to describe the system model in terms of the functions (outputs) to be met and system implementation in terms of programs, files, and so on. The total process extends over six steps, beginning with the identification of the actions and entities and ending with the implementation of the system.

1.5.5 Higher-Order Software

Higher-order software (HOS) cannot really be defined as a design technique. What is it, then? It really is software that was designed by two brilliant mathematicians, Margaret Hamilton and Saydean Zeldin, to provide programs in which the logic could be proven to be mathematically correct. Hamilton and Zeldin have formed a company called Higher-Order Software, Inc., which markets HOS. HOS can be applied without any knowledge of the complex mathematics used to develop the product. The authors claim that all that is required is a two-day course. An organization using HOS would gradually build up a library of modules and programs that could be used over and over again. The mathematics of HOS is based on binary tree structures in which each node represents a function. These trees are built up using three primitive control structures, Join, Include, and Or.

James Martin describes HOS in *Program Design Which is Provably Correct*, published by Savant. There he describes the principles involved in the software design and the process to be followed to use it. The book is very easy to read and to follow. Any organization considering the acquisition of HOS or interested in learning more about it would be well advised to obtain a copy and read it.

1.5.6 Prototyping

In computerese the term *prototyping* rolls off the tongue and conveys the impression that prototypes can be easily built, particularly by using powerful fourth-generation programming languages. These prototypes can be handed to the system designers and analysts, who will convert them to systems which will then meet the user's real requirements precisely. Or, alternatively, designers and analysts can develop prototype outputs on screens using software which provides a screen specification which can be inserted in a program that uses the screen. Sounds great! Unfortunately, much of this is "pie in the sky." No system worth the name can be built without a specification, no more than a house can be built using prefabricated materials without a plan. Chapter 9 discusses how systems can be designed and built effectively combining the system specification and design techniques with the powerful prototyping tools available in the market today.

1.6 OTHER TOPICS TO BE COVERED

1.6.1 Specification and Design Techniques and Application
System Development Methodologies

This book would not be complete if the impact of information system design and specification techniques on application system development methodologies (ASDMs) were not considered. There are numerous ASDMs on the market and many more have been developed in-house. It is assumed, particularly by senior management, that an ASDM is a project management tool and hence that a particular ASDM installed in an organization can be used with every system specification and design technique. This is only partially true. This subject is discussed in Chapter 10, where an approach is recommended to solve the problem.

1.6.2 Data Use Analysis

Data use analysis is an information engineering activity. It is dealt with in a separate chapter, as every information system design should be complemented with a physical file or data-base design. The physical data-base or file design is affected by the volume of data to be stored and the number of accesses to the data base. Chapter 11 describes how the volumes and the accesses can be analyzed.

1.6.3 The Information Explosion

The final chapter in the book examines some combinations of system specification and design techniques. The book ends with some thoughts on where business system design may be headed in the future.

1.7 STUDYING THIS BOOK

This book contains a large amount of information and covers a variety of topics. It is possible that readers may feel they are being subjected to an "information overload" and be put off from studying it in depth. To get the maximum benefit from the material in the text, I recommend that readers go through it quickly to obtain an overview. They can then concentrate on those chapters which are of particular interest. It is very unlikely that any reader will attempt to apply all the techniques described. The most effective approach would be to select one technique and apply it successfully before attempting to apply a second.

To make this book more challenging for the reader who wishes to practice some of the theories described here, the case study has been described in considerable detail in the narrative and in the accompanying diagrams. In addition, the chapter on information engineering contains considerable information on the system's data. On the other hand, the case-study examples supporting the techniques are described only to the extent necessary to explain the theory. This provides readers with ample scope to apply their newly acquired knowledge to other facets of the case study. In many instances they will find that there is a lot of work to be done, and what may appear easy or simplistic in theory is much more difficult to apply in practice.

This book is not intended to be sexist in any shape or form. I use the male pronoun throughout to include both men and women. I hope that readers will accept this approach.

2

The Case Study
Description

2.1 THE LIBRARY SYSTEM

The case study described in this chapter and used throughout the text is based on a real-life system. This has certain advantages, as the problems and the needs identified are not theoretical and hence include complexities and peculiarities that can occur in the real world. On the other hand, the problems and needs may not cover every contingency that should be examined during a discussion of the techniques. When this type of situation arises, the discussion is supported by other appropriate examples.

As this book is about information system specification and design, the reader should be able to relate to a library situated in a systems department that provides a library service to the department staff and to users outside. This library is responsible for all systems documentation, the computer mainframe supplier's publications, all reports produced internally and externally, all administrative and technical manuals, reference material, newspapers and periodicals, forms used in the department, and stationery supplies. The case study deals specifically with the library's documentation and report needs, although the actual system covers the entire library.

System size and complexity are difficult to measure. Is size based on the number of lines of code, or is it based on the number of records processed? Is an interactive on-line system more complex than a batch system? Is a distributed system more complex than a centralized system? What is the difference between a large system and a small one? I raise these issues because it is often stated that such and such system was easy to design, build, and implement because it was "small" or because it was not "complex"; or the examples provided in the "text" were simplistic and things are far more complex in real life. Rather than discuss the Library System's size and complexity, the following statistics should provide the reader with a perspective of the system.

2.2 SYSTEM STATISTICS

Number of documentation binders (volumes)	5000
Number of archival documents (reports, etc.)	500
Number of copies of administrative and technical manuals	1000
Number of reference books	200
Number of periodicals and newspapers	600
Number of mainframe supplier publications	1500
Number of systems-related forms	200
Number of stationery items	100
Number of daily transactions processed, including new material received, updates received, loans (charge-outs), returns (charge-ins), manual updates issued, and so on	300
Total file storage required (megabytes)	5
Number of management control reports produced monthly	30
Number of storage locations [includes primary storage (in department), secure storage (external secure building), and secondary storage (external building)]	3

2.3 HISTORY

The library came into being in the 1950s when computer systems were first introduced into the organization. It was primarily a repository for any program documentation that might have been produced. In the mid-1970s, the importance of documentation and security was realized and the library became a more formal organizational entity. A supervisor was appointed and a procedure manual developed. When the computer system was being developed, the library staff consisted of one supervisor and five librarians.

2.4 PROBLEMS ENCOUNTERED

In order to control the large volume of material stored in the library and to process the daily transactions, a number of registers and logs were set up. The data were often duplicated and even triplicated, resulting in copying errors, which in turn required checking and redoing. Further, the management reports needed to measure service and throughput took considerable amounts of time. It was decided that the current system was inadequate and had to be replaced. The alternatives considered were: (1) a redesigned manual system and (2) an interactive on-line system. Taking into account the increased accuracy that could be achieved by entering data once only and the possible labor savings, it was decided to build the computer system.

2.5 SYSTEM DOCUMENTATION AND ARCHIVAL DOCUMENTS PROCESSING

Any document received in the library has a certain life cycle. During that life cycle, it is subject to specific actions. These are registration, processing, filing, lending, obsoletion, and destruction. The tasks associated with each activity vary depending on the type of document. As the discussion of the techniques is restricted to system documentation and archival documents, the tasks associated with them are described below and in Figures 2.1 to 2.10.

2.5.1 System Documentation

The systems analyst/programmer compiles the system documentation according to the requirements of the documentation standards being followed. The documentation may reside in one or more binders or volumes. The analyst/programmer submits it to the library together with a form called a *Delivery Notice*, which contains information about the document.

> *Registration:* The librarian compares the Delivery Notice to the document and if the two match, enters the document's name and number in the Daily Register. He also files the Delivery Notice in the Delivery Notice file.

> *Processing:* The librarian makes a photocopy of the document for secure storage, enters the document data in both the On-Site and Off-Site Documentation Indexes, creates a form called a *History Log* and attaches a copy to the front of both the original and the photo-

copy, makes up a Charge-out (loan) Card for the Charge-out Register, and enters the document information in the Document Processed Log. He enters the photocopy data in the Documents Shipped Off-Site Register and ships the copy off-site to the secure storage location.

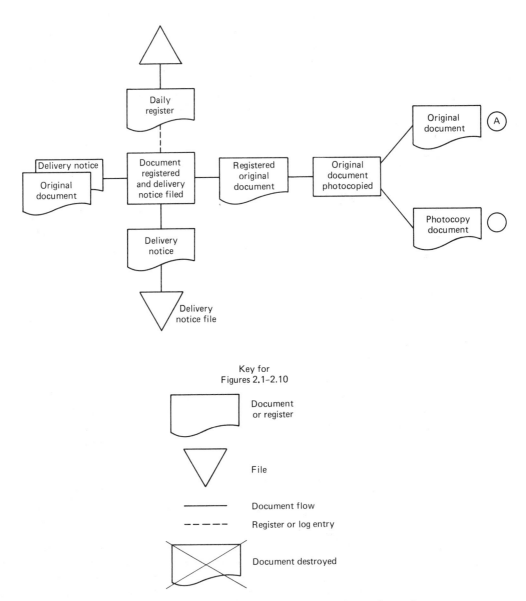

Figure 2.1 System documentation registration and copying.

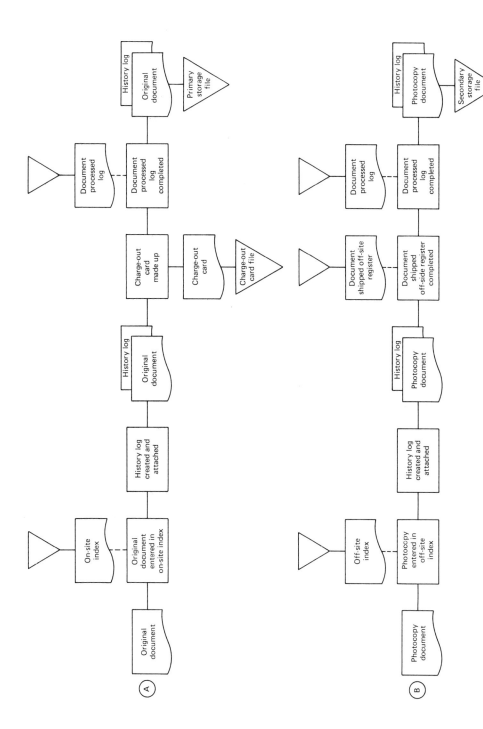

Figure 2.2 System documentation processing and filing.

Filing: The librarian files the original documentation in primary storage and the photocopy in secure storage.

Lending (Charging out): When a request is received for a document, the librarian loans the document and the loan is recorded on the Charge-out Card. When the document is returned, the librarian records the return (charge-in) on the Charge-out Card and files the document.

Obsoletion: When a document is made obsolete (this can occur for a variety of reasons, e.g., the system is rebuilt, the operating system changes, etc.), the librarian enters the obsoletion data (Retention Period and Reason Obsoleted) in the On-Site and Off-Site Indexes, enters the original documentation data in the Documents Shipped Off-Site Register, ships the original to secure storage, and destroys the photocopy.

Destruction: When the retention period expires, the librarian destroys the original documentation and updates the Off-Site Index.

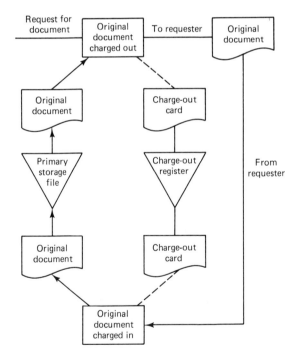

Figure 2.3 System documentation charging (lending).

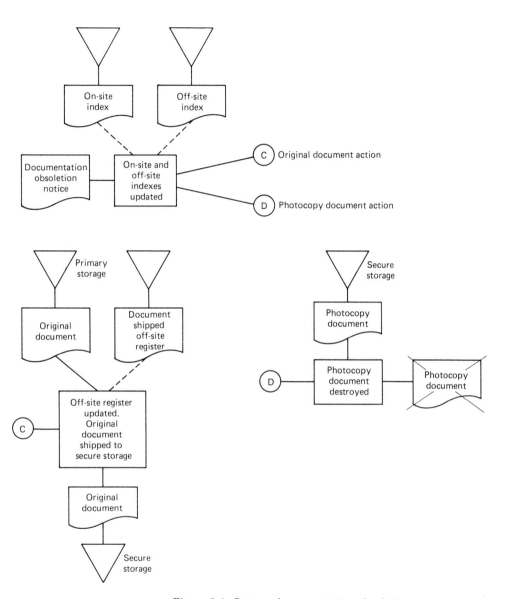

Figure 2.4 System documentation obsoletion.

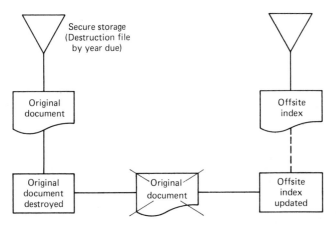

Figure 2.5 System documentation destruction.

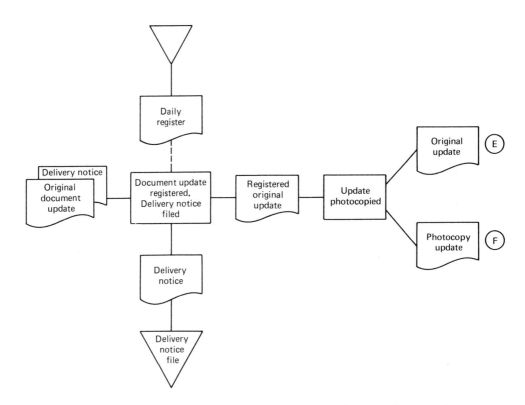

Figure 2.6 System documentation update registration and photocopying.

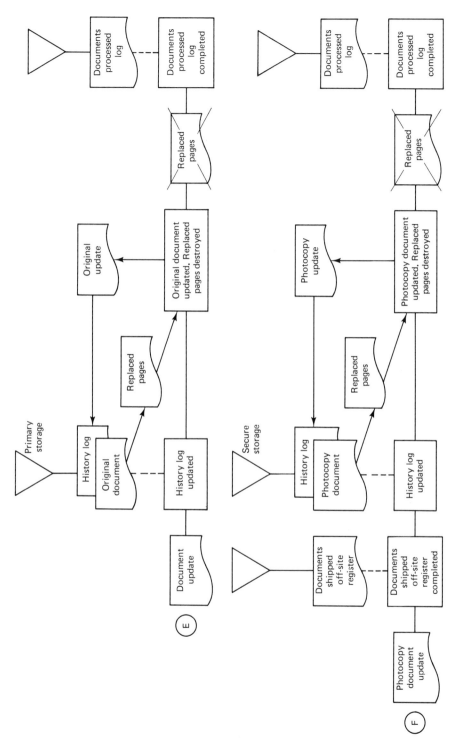

Figure 2.7 System documentation update processing and filing.

2.5.2 System Documentation Update

When the systems analyst/programmer makes a change to a system, he updates the documentation and submits the update to the library together with a Delivery Notice.

Registration: The librarian registers the update and files the Delivery Notice.

Processing: The librarian makes a photocopy of the update for secure storage, enters the update data in the original document's History Log and the Document Processed Log, and completes the Documents Shipped Off-Site Register. He ships the copy off-site to the secure storage location, where he updates the photocopy document's History Log.

Filing: The librarian inserts the update in the original and photocopy of the documentation and destroys any pages that have been replaced.

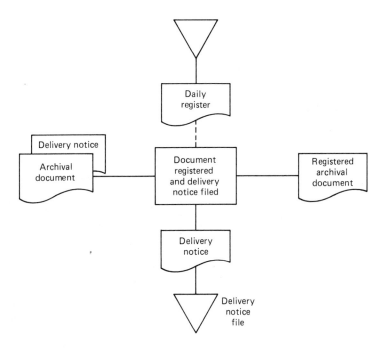

Figure 2.8 Archival document registration.

2.5.3 Archival Documents

Archival documents are any reports that are filed in the library. Such reports could include requests for proposals from vendors, equipment evaluations, and so on. They are called *archival documents* because they are retained for a specified period and are not updated. They are generally sent to the library after they have been actioned and are no longer required. They, too, are accompanied by a Delivery Notice.

Registration: The librarian registers the archival document and files the Delivery Notice.

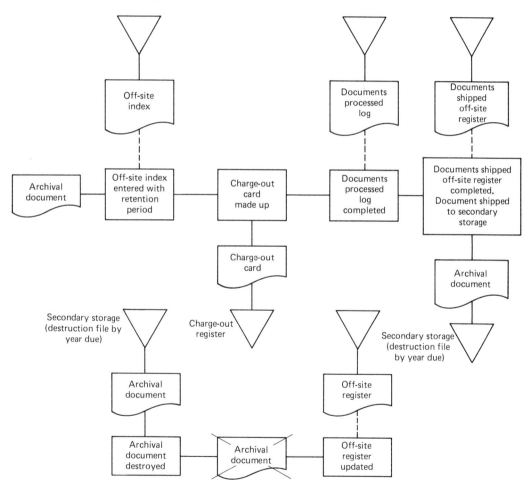

Figure 2.9 Archival document processing, filing, and destruction.

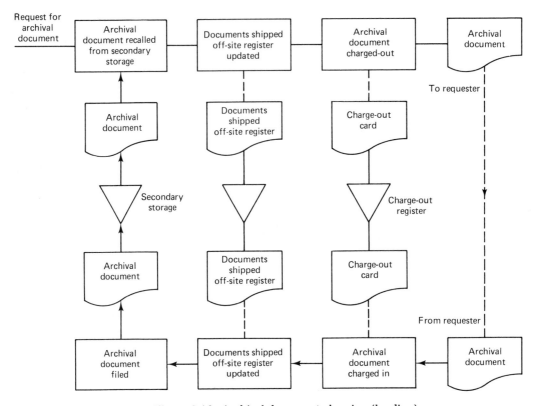

Figure 2.10 Archival document charging (lending).

Processing: The librarian makes up a Charge-out Card, completes the Document Processed Log, the Documents Shipped Off-Site Register, and the Off-Site Index and ships the document off-site to secondary storage.

Filing: The librarian files the document in secondary storage.

Lending (Charging out): When a request is received for a report, the librarian recalls the document from the off-site location and loans it to the person who is requesting it. The loan is entered on the Charge-out card. When the document is returned, the librarian charges it in and ships it to the off-site location, where he files it again.

Destruction: When the retention period expires, the librarian destroys the document and updates the Off-Site Index.

The Basic Components of a Business Information System

Before we begin to delve into the depths of the system specification and design techniques, we should establish the scope of this book. Computer systems can be designed and built to serve a million and one needs. These can vary from the very common business information needs to missile guidance and satellite control. In between, systems can be built to regulate elevators in high-rise buildings, traffic control, assembly line parts scheduling, and for many other uses. We are concerned here with business systems only. These systems serve the information needs of management's strategic, tactical, and operational objectives. In other words, they provide decision-making, operating, and control information. They can range from long-term forecasts to depositing money in a bank across the counter or by computerized teller. All these business applications have certain features in common.

Every system can be considered a black box which has input, process, files, and output. The basic difference between a business system and any other is that the majority of the business systems' outputs are in the form of information (formatted data) printed in reports, invoices, screens, checks, and so on, while most other systems' outputs are not printed information. For example, an elevator system's output is to bring the elevator to the appropriate floor, a missile guidance system's output is to keep the missile on target, and a traffic control system's output is to regulate the traffic lights to fit best the flow of traffic.

Returning to the basic components of a system, we have data input, data stored, data processed, and data output, as shown in Figure 3.1. The conventional approach to information system design, regardless of the

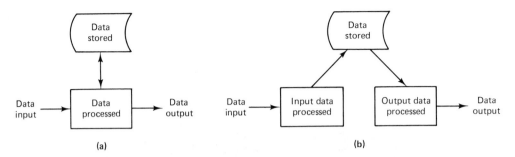

Figure 3.1 A system as a "Black Box."

technique, is that data are input to a process which reads the data stored in files, updates the files, and produces the data output. By implication, data can be output from the process which do not have to be recorded in any file. For example, a program or module could have a table of data element values embedded in it. Such data are integral to the process and the data and process cannot be separated. These data are called *internal variables.* Such systems are usually difficult to maintain because a change in program logic could change or lose internal variables. This could result in a chain reaction through other programs or modules, causing totally unexpected problems. An even greater disadvantage is that there is no audit trail to follow through the files.

To overcome this problem, systems can be designed so that inputs *only* update files and files *only* produce outputs. Now we have five components in a basic computer system: data input, data input processed, data stored, data output processed, and the data output [see Figure 3.1]. The distinction between the data input processed and the data output processed enables us to look at system design in two parts: file maintenance and output production.

3.1 DATA INPUT

Data input to a computer must be structured (organized) so that they can be accepted by the computer. Data are normally grouped into sets or chains called *records.* Figure 3.2, for example, is an Invoice Header record. Each record has a set of *data elements.* In the Invoice Header, the data elements (also called *data attributes*) are Invoice Number, Company Name, and Company Address. Each data element has a certain length, consisting of characters similar to the characters on a typewriter (e.g., letters, numerals, punctuation marks, and mathematical and miscellaneous symbols.)

Each record has at least one *key* (i.e., the data element or elements that identify it). In the example, the Invoice Number is the key. Hence the addition of an Invoice Header record implies the addition of the Invoice

Invoice number	Company name	Company address

Figure 3.2 Example of a simple record.

Number key; the deletion of the record implies the deletion of the key; and the modification of the record implies the addition, deletion, or change to Company Name and/or Company Address. Records input to a computer can be entered singly (e.g., through a terminal) or grouped using a file containing a number of identical records.

3.2 DATA STORED

Data can be stored in a variety of ways and in a variety of structures. From the user's viewpoint, the data are either in *random access storage* such as disk files, or in *batch storage* such as tape files. Records in a file can be *independent* or *dependent* on one another in a hierarchy or a network.

In Figure 3.3, the two sets of records for the Invoice Header and the Line Item contain the same data. In fact, the Invoice Header record is the same in both examples. The difference is in the Line Item records. The first Line Item record is independent because it has Invoice Number as part of the key. The second record is dependent on the Invoice Header because the link indicates that the Line Item is part of a particular invoice whose Invoice Number is found in the Invoice Header.

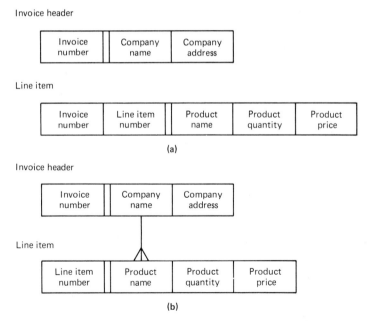

Figure 3.3 (a) Independent and (b) dependent data.

3.2.1 Types of File/Data-Base Structures

A *hierarchy* is a family tree of records, with any parent record having one or more children records which are dependent on the parent keys. A *network* consists of a file with individual records linked in pairs. A *set of relations* consists of independent records linked through relational algebra or calculus. These three structures are used in the three types of data-base management systems commonly available. All other files are basically flat files (i.e., files with independent records). Readers who wish to explore the different types of data-base management systems in depth may refer to James Martin's *Computer Data-Base Organization*.

3.3 OUTPUT DATA

Output data are data that are read by people. As such, they must be presented to the reader in a format and structure that he can use. Any output record may have the same structure as a record in the file, be part of a file record, or could result from data combined from two or more records in the file. The records could also be derived. For example, column totals may not reside in the file but could be calculated during the output process. (The reader should not confuse records which are derivatives of records in files with output records, which are integral to an input process. The latter provide feedback on data acceptance only, such as the message "No matching record found.")

3.4 FILE MAINTENANCE

File maintenance is the processing of input data to update the data stored in the files. (The term *file* includes data-base management systems.) The programs or modules maintain each record in the file or files individually. Each input record's content and structure are read and matched with the record definition in the program or data-base management system. If it does not match the record definition, it will be rejected. If it matches the record definition, it could be further validated with criteria established in the program or module. Assuming that it is a valid record, it may then update a record in file or combine with other input data and/or records in file and update a particular record. Human-readable output data obtained during file maintenance should relate only to information regarding acceptance or rejection of the input data. (These output data are not to be confused with the data obtained during output production.)

The basic functions performed during file maintenance are:

- Addition of records
- Deletion of records

- Modification of records (i.e., the addition, deletion, or the updating of data elements)
- Reading (accessing) data in a record without updating them

These additions, deletions, modifications, and accesses are called *Events*. The following example illustrates these functions.

Example 1

An Orders file contains the following records (keys are underlined):

- Customer (Customer Number, Customer Name, Customer Address)
- Order Header (Order Number, Customer Number)
- Product (Product Number, Product Name, Product Price, Quantity in Stock)
- Order Item [Line Item in the order] (Order Number, Item Number, Product Number, Quantity Ordered)

When an order for stock is received, the events that occur are:

1. The Customer record input is validated (Customer is read).
2. An invalid Customer record is rejected.
3. An Order Header record is set up (Order Header is added).
4. The Product ordered is validated (Product is read).
5. An invalid Product is rejected.
6. An Order Item is set up (Order Item is added).
7. The Stock is verified (Product is read).
8. The Stock is reduced (Product is modified).

A conclusion that can be drawn from Example 1 is that in file maintenance, highly functional modules can be designed where each module executes a single, basic event (i.e., add, delete, modify, or retrieve records). The only additional functions the modules should be designed to perform are the necessary validations and computations required to update a particular record. We will return to the development of these modules in the discussion of the various system design techniques.

3.5 OUTPUT PRODUCTION

In output production, programs or modules take data (without removing or changing them) from a file or files and produce "reports," such as video screens, invoices, checks, control reports, and files. The latter files could be input to other file maintenance or could be printed. Referring back to Example 1, the order could be printed with the order header and several line items or a list of stock reductions could be produced.

It is worth emphasizing that by dividing the data processed into file maintenance and output production, the updating of the files has been completely separated from the production of output. Also, the production of a single report or a set of reports during one output production process is completely independent of every similar output production process.

Before the reader concludes that file maintenance and output production must always be in separate programs, it should be noted that a program may contain both features. What is essential is that the modules within the program not combine the two features. This is illustrated using our Orders example:

File maintenance

Add Order Header; includes validation of Customer Number.	Read Order Header record input. Validate Customer Number. Reject invalid Customer Number. Establish Order Header.
Add Order item; includes Product validation and verification of Stock Quantity.	Read Order Item record input. Validate Product Number. Reject invalid Product Number. Verify Quantity in Stock greater than Quantity Ordered. Reject if insufficient Quantity in Stock. Establish Order Item.
Modify Quantity in Stock.	Reduce Quantity in Stock. Repeat Read of Order Item record until no more Order Items.

Output production

Retrieve Customer Name and Customer Address (from Customer record).
Print Order Header.
Retrieve Product Name and Product Price (from Product record).
Compute Total Product Cost.
Print Order Item.
Compute Order Cost.
Print Order Cost.
Compute Tax 7% of Order Cost.
Print Tax.
Compute Total Order Cost.
Print Total Order Cost.

The program above has two distinct parts: a file maintenance part and an output production part. The file maintenance part consists of a series of

modules that execute add, read, and modify events combined with validations and computations. The output production part is one module that
produces the report.

3.6 FILE/DATA-BASE CONTENT AND STRUCTURE

Based on the discussion above, we could conclude that the effectiveness of
a system in meeting the user's needs is directly dependent on the right
data being present in the files and the files being organized to make the
production of outputs as simple as possible.

It also follows that changing the file's content or organization has
a direct impact on file maintenance and output production. So if a file
is well designed in terms of the user's functional needs, it should not be
necessary to change it unless the user's functions change. If a file does
change, it should not be difficult to make the corresponding changes in the
related modules and programs.

3.7 SYSTEMS, PROGRAMS, AND MODULES

We may appear to be putting the cart before the horse. The terms *system*,
program, and *module* have been used freely to this point without discussing
what they mean. The assumption made was that the reader had some expo-
sure to system design and hence could recognize the terms. Before we proceed any further, however, let us define them so that when they are referred
to in the text, you will know how they are being used.

System: a set of processes that meets specific needs. These processes
require input and provide output to meet these needs. Systems exist
everywhere and the world would collapse if nature did not operate very
effective systems. Our interest in this text is restricted to information
systems. Information systems exist to satisfy specific management
policies. We view information systems in terms of manual processes
and computer processes. In fact, we assume that every process not
carried out on the computer is manual. For example, a person operating a mailing machine is considered to be executing a manual process
even though the machine is doing the work. A computer system consists of a set of programs, input data, stored data, and output data.

Program: a physical entity in a computer system which can stand
alone. It has a specific name by which it is called or accessed from a
library. It has a fixed physical organization. In COBOL, for example,
it has an identification division, a data division, a working storage
section, a linkage section, and a procedure division. It can talk to the

operating system (the system that makes the computer function). It generally consists of a set of physical modules. It, too, can be considered to be a system, but a system with limited functions.

Module: a set of computer instructions that executes instructions on data input and produces data as output. A *physical module* consists of one or more *logical modules.* When this occurs, the logical modules are said to be "packaged." A logical module, which is a set of instructions that executes logical functions, cannot be stored or accessed. A physical module can be stored in a library and can be called by a program or another physical module when it is to be executed.

REFERENCE

1. James Martin, *Computer Data-Base Organization,* 2nd ed., Prentice-Hall, Inc., Englewood Cliffs, NJ, 1977.

Information
Engineering

4.1 WHAT IS INFORMATION ENGINEERING?

Information engineering is a term coined by James Martin and Clive Finkelstein [1] to encompass a set of disciplines that effectively satisfy an organization's mission and objectives. Systems built using information engineering
are

- Based on data and data relationships which are independent of process
  flow but are dependent on business policy.
- User driven; that is, systems development staff members play only
  supporting roles during the logical system specification and design
  process.

The management disciplines that make up information engineering include:

- Strategic requirements planning
- Information analysis with data modeling and canonical synthesis
- Procedure formation
- Data use analysis
- Implementation strategies
- Distribution analysis
- Physical data-base design

- Fourth-generation languages
- Program specification synthesis

These are shown in Figure 4.1.

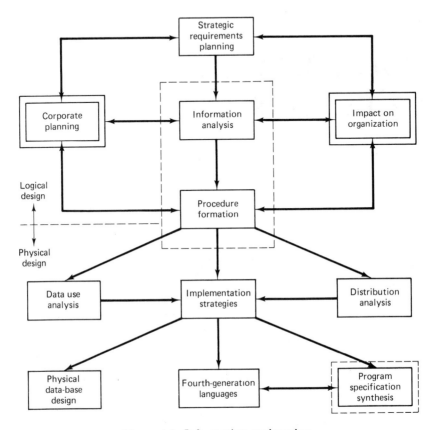

Figure 4.1 Information engineering.

4.2 OVERVIEW OF THE INFORMATION ENGINEERING DISCIPLINES

Strategic requirements planning is the establishment of long-range plans based on the organization's purpose and mission supported by its long-range strategic objectives, and the identification of information to meet present and future needs.

Information analysis includes the definition of tactical and operational objectives and the information needed to meet these objectives. Taking into account current data in use, this information is translated into stable, logical data models which display the organization's entities and their associations.

(As the term *entity* has different meanings when used by different authors, it is appropriate to define the term each time it is used in a different context.)

> *Entity:* In information engineering, an entity is something that exists in the real world outside the computer system and is reflected in the data model. Examples from the Library System include System Documentation, Users, and Loans (Charge-outs). These entities can become records later with keys and data elements or attributes.

Procedure formation is a technique for defining business procedures based on the stable business data model developed in information analysis. The users analyze the entities or records in the data model and identify events that add, delete, modify, or access each entity or record. At the same time, they identify the conditions that precede or succeed events. The combination of events and conditions provides the basis for the logic used in the system's computer and manual procedures.

Data use analysis is the analysis of the stable data model in terms of the accesses through the model resulting from the procedures and the record volumes anticipated. This information is used in the design of the physical data bases or files. Since physical file design is part of the implementation process for every system, regardless of the system design technique used, data use analysis is dealt with in a separate chapter (Chapter 11).

Implementation strategies are used to implement the system design. They include processes such as testing, hardware and software specification and acquisition, and program libraries.

Distribution analysis is the analysis of the corporate data requirements to determine whether data bases or files should be centralized or distributed, the structure and content of the different data bases or files, the communication networks and the data dictionary controls required, and so on.

Physical data-base design is the design of the physical data bases and files based on the business data model, data use analysis, and the physical data-base and file environment available in the organization.

Fourth-generation languages are nonprocedural languages in which the developer states "what is required from the process" rather than "how the process flows." Examples of fourth-generation languages are FOCUS, NOMAD, and RAMIS. Examples of procedural languages are PL/1, COBOL, and BASIC. The use of fourth-generation languages results in code which is simpler and less prone to error than the code produced using tools such as COBOL. However, they are not a panacea and come in different forms to meet different needs. Often, they need to be supplemented by procedural languages to deal with special situations.

Program specification synthesis is a technique used to produce program code using predefined common modules which are identified in a data dictionary. The common modules are predefined based on the procedures developed during procedure formation. It is assumed that these modules have been tested and are error free. The majority of these modules relate to the addition, deletion, modification, and referencing of records.

In this chapter only those disciplines that directly affect the system design are discussed. These are information analysis, procedure formation, and program specification synthesis. They are shown enclosed by dashed lines in Figure 4.1

4.3 INFORMATION ANALYSIS

The output from information analysis is a stable data model which reflects both management's information needs based on their strategic, tactical, and operational requirements, and data currently produced and used in the organization. This data model is used during procedure formation to develop computer and manual procedures, and during data use analysis to develop the specifications for the physical data base or files.

James Martin and Clive Finkelstein advocate approaches to information analysis which differ slightly. In *Information Engineering* [1], information analysis produces a high-level data model which is partitioned to enable each partition to be "canonically synthesized" separately. The output from canonical synthesis is the stable data model. In the six articles published in *Computerworld* magazine [2], Finkelstein describes information analysis as a process that begins with objectives' definition and includes all the steps associated with the development of the stable data model. With apologies to Martin and Finkelstein, the ten steps described in Section 4.3.2 are slightly different from both their approaches, but the final outcome is the same.

The canonical synthesis approach to normalization of the data model is described by Martin in several of his books, including *Information Engineering* [1] and *Computer Data-Base Organization* [3]. This subject is covered in Section 4.4. I promised the reader earlier that any jargon or use of words with different meanings would be explained as they were encountered. The word *canonical* is defined in *Webster's New Collegiate Dictionary* (1974) as "reduced to the simplest or clearest schema possible." The same dictionary defines *schema* as a "diagrammatic presentation," in this context, a diagrammatic presentation of the data required by any user to meet a specific need (e.g., to produce a specific report). *Normalization* is a term coined by E. F. Codd [4] in the context of canonical data structures. It is best explained by illustration.

4.3.1 Data Normalization

A *normalized record* can be described as a record which is independent and stable. It is independent because it has no external dependencies, and it is stable because it is in its simplest form. Normalization is most often carried out in three stages, each of which is termed a *normal form.* The process can be extended further, but from a practical viewpoint, three normal forms are adequate.

4.3.1.1 **First normal form.**   Consider the following Documentation Volume record. It contains data identifying a specific volume of documentation and its updates. The keys are underlined. The update data are in the form of a *repeating group.* (Repeating groups are used in all hierarchical data-base systems. An example that we encountered earlier was the dependent data Line Item described in Section 3.2.)

Documentation volume

<u>Documentation</u> <u>Identification</u> <u>Number</u>, <u>Documentation</u> <u>Volume</u> <u>Number</u>, Documentation Name, Type of Access, Date Written Notice to Obsolete Received, Obsoletion Date, Date Obsoleted, Retention Period, Term of Loan, Date Received, Date Processed, Date Filed, Individual Prepared By, Individual Prepared By's Department, Submitted By, Date Destroyed, Destroyed By (<u>Documentation</u> <u>Update</u> <u>Serial</u> <u>Number</u>, Prepared By, Submitted By, Date Received, Date Processed, Date Filed, Filed By)

In first normal form, we eliminate all repeating groups. The Documentation Volume record has only one such group relating to "updates" (the data elements within parentheses). We now have two records:

Documentation volume

<u>Documentation</u> <u>Identification</u> <u>Number</u>, <u>Documentation</u> <u>Volume</u> <u>Number</u>, Documentation Name, Type of Access, Date Written Notice to Obsolete Received, Obsoletion Date, Date Obsoleted, Retention Period, Term of Loan, Date Received, Date Processed, Date Filed, Individual Prepared By, Individual Prepared By's Department, Submitted By, Date Destroyed, Destroyed By

Documentation volume update

<u>Documentation</u> <u>Identification</u> <u>Number</u>, <u>Documentation</u> <u>Volume</u> <u>Number</u>, <u>Documentation</u> <u>Update</u> <u>Serial</u> <u>Number</u>, Prepared By, Submitted By, Date Received, Date Processed, Date Filed, Filed By

4.3.1.2 Second normal form.   In *second normal form*, every data element in a record must be dependent on every data element in the primary key. The primary key of the first-normal-form version of the Documentation Volume record has two data elements, Documentation Identification Number and Documentation Volume Number. The following table shows the data elements and their dependencies on the two keys.

Data element	Documentation identification number	Documentation volume number
Documentation Name	*	
Type of Access	*	
Date Written	*	
Notice to Obsolete Received		
Obsoletion Date	*	
Date Obsoleted	*	
Retention Period	*	
Term of Loan	*	
Date Received		*
Date Processed		*
Date Filed		*
Individual Prepared By		*
Individual Prepared By's Department		*
Submitted By		*
Date Destroyed		*
Destroyed By		*

Now we have three records in second normal form:

Documentation

Documentation Identification Number, Documentation Name, Type of Access, Date Written Notice to Obsolete Received, Obsoletion Date, Date Obsoleted, Retention Period, Term of Loan

Documentation volume

Documentation Identification Number, Documentation Volume Number, Date Received, Date Processed, Date Filed, Individual Prepared By, Individual Prepared By's Department, Submitted By, Date Destroyed, Destroyed By

Documentation volume update

<u>Documentation</u> <u>Identification</u> <u>Number</u>, <u>Documentation</u> <u>Volume</u> <u>Number</u>, <u>Documentation</u> <u>Update</u> <u>Serial</u> <u>Number</u>, Prepared By, Submitted By, Date Received, Date Processed, Date Filed, Filed By

Before moving on to third normal form, let us examine the Documentation Volume Update record. Documentation updates relate to documentation as a whole because a single update could affect more than one volume. Under these conditions, the analyst may choose to modify the record and have it relate to documentation as a whole rather than the volume of documentation. If this were to occur, Documentation Volume Number would be deleted from the key.

4.3.1.3 Third normal form. In third normal form, no data element should be dependent on any other data element which is not part of the primary key. In the Documentation Volume record in second normal form, Individual Prepared By's Department is dependent only on Individual Prepared By and is not dependent on either of the data elements in the primary key. This gives us a fourth record:

Individual prepared by

<u>Individual</u> <u>Prepared</u> <u>By</u>, Individual Prepared By's Department

Documentation Volume becomes:

Documentation volume

<u>Documentation</u> <u>Identification</u> <u>Number</u>, <u>Documentation</u> <u>Volume</u> <u>Number</u>, Date Received, Date Processed, Date Filed, Individual Prepared By, Submitted By, Date Destroyed, Destroyed By

On completion of normalization, the four records in third normal form are Documentation, Documentation Volume, Documentation Volume Update, and Individual Prepared By.

4.3.1.4 Projection and join. The end result of data model normalization is a stable set of records which can provide the user with any information he requires to meet his objectives. This information may be obtained from complete records, parts of records, or combinations of records. When an output record is produced which is part of a record in the model, it is called a *projection*. When two records are combined to produce a third, it is called a *join*. Consider the following records:

Archival document reference

<u>Archival</u> <u>Document</u> <u>Name</u>, <u>Archival</u> <u>Document</u> <u>Copy</u> <u>Number</u>, User Identification Number, Date Requested, Authorized By, Date Retrieved, Date Referenced, Date Reshipped Off-Site, Date Refiled

User

<u>User</u> <u>Identification</u> <u>Number</u>, Name, Title, Phone Number

A user wants a report that lists all archival documents which took more than five days from the date requested to the date retrieved. The record output would be a projection from Archival Document Reference. It would be as follows:

<u>Archival</u> <u>Document</u> <u>Name</u>, <u>Archival</u> <u>Document</u> <u>Copy</u> <u>Number</u>, Date Requested, Date Retrieved

The same user also wants a list of persons by name and by title who referenced a particular archival document in January 1983. The result would be a join of Archival Document Reference and User on the data element User Identification Number. The output record would be as follows:

<u>User</u> <u>Identification</u> <u>Number</u>, Name, Title, Date Referenced

4.3.1.5 Insufficient data description. This output record highlights a possible problem that could occur through insufficient data element description. Date Referenced was meaningful as long as it was part of the Archival Document Reference record. As soon as it was removed from this record, it was no longer meaningful (i.e., Date Referenced could be understood to relate to Documentation as much as to Archival Document). Hence the data element should be described as Archival Document Date Referenced.

4.3.1.6 Primary and secondary records. Records that are defined in a normalized data model may be termed *primary records*. They are primary because they are essential and if removed from the model would result in the user's needs not being met. *Secondary records* are records that can be derived every time a program is executed, but doing so incurs an unnecessary overhead. An example of a secondary record is a Month-to-Date Balance. This can be calculated each month from the beginning of the year, but it is far simpler to add the current month's total to the balance from the previous month's. Jean D. Warnier discusses this approach in the *Logical Construction of Systems* [5]. (Although Warnier's file design techniques are not discussed in this book, the reader may find some of his ideas well worth examining.)

The best way to identify secondary records is to obtain them from the output reports the system will produce. They could be a by-product of canonical synthesis or be identified when the output reports are defined. The appropriate time to include them in the data model is just prior to data use analysis. The reader should remember to identify them in the data dictionary as secondary records and to put them aside before making any changes in the normalized data model.

4.3.1.7 Derived records.   A file or data base built from a normalized data model will not contain every output record that may possibly be required. These records should be defined in the output programs that produce them.

4.3.1.8 Conversion of a normalized data model to a physical data base.   In a normalized data model, each record is independent of every other record. So, in essence, the data model is relational and can be converted to a relational data base without further change. Grouping records linked by arrows in pairs converts the model to a CODASYL data base. A hierarchical data base is obtained by defining the dependencies between records (i.e., by removing the keys of the parent record from the child record). The Invoice Header and Line Item records in Section 3.2 illustrate dependent and independent records. This subject is discussed in depth by James Martin in *Computer Data-Base Organization* [3].

4.3.2 Ten Steps in Information Analysis

The ten steps in information analysis are:

1. Define the organization's or business application's objectives.
2. Identify the information required to meet the objectives.
3. Prepare the data model.
4. Expand data on the data dictionary.
5. Partition the data model.
6. Normalize the data.
7. Examine current data.
8. Resolve data conflicts.
9. Finalize data normalization and complete the data model.
10. Cross-check the data model and objectives.

Step 1: Define the organization's or business application's objectives.

Strategic requirements planning defines the organization's mission and purpose, and its strategic, long-term objectives. Tactical requirements planning looks at objectives that can be budgeted on a one- to two-year basis, and operational planning looks at objectives in terms of needs to be met daily, weekly, and monthly. All these objectives can be measured using:

- Decision-making information
- Control information
- Operational information

The setting of objectives in any organization and at any level is a difficult exercise. Few organizations set formal objectives of any kind. To expect an organization to identify the need and to carry out this task at the strategic, tactical, and operational levels without further ado is to display a large measure of naivety. Further, to expect a systems analyst to define objectives for the user verges on the absurd. Only the user can define his own objectives. An astute analyst may be able to assist him, particularly at the operational level.

Information analysis can be done at any level in an organization from the corporate level to the business application level. The higher the level, the broader the scope of the data model and the possible need to expand it more than once. In our case study, we have defined operational objectives at the business application level only. Table 4.1 lists the Library System objectives.

TABLE 4.1 LIBRARY SYSTEM OBJECTIVES

---

1. Make systems documentation and documentation updates available for reference and charge-out within two working days from date of receipt in the library.
2. Make documentation obsolete within seven working days from date of written notice to obsolete received in the library.
3. Ship weekly all documentation updates, backup photocopies of documentation, and archival documents to secure or secondary storage.
4. Update and file monthly all documentation updates, photocopies of documentation, and archival documents in secure or secondary storage.
5. Conduct an audit of off-site documentation semiannually to verify that off-site documentation and on-site documentation are identical.
6. Make obsolete all archival documents scheduled for obsoletion within thirty days of the obsoletion date.
7. Retrieve any document requested from off-site storage within two working days of the receipt of the request.
8. Ensure that only authorized users reference or borrow documentation or archival documents from the library.
9. Follow-up on all charge-outs that extend over one month.

Step 2: Identify the information required to meet the objectives.

This step can be subdivided into the identification of the data required to meet each objective and the reorganization of these data into logical entities.

The terms *logical* and *physical* have been used earlier but were not explained. When something is described as being *logical*, it means that its different parts are linked together by logic. When something is described as being *physical*, it means that the parts are linked together so that they will work on a computer. For example, in Section 3.5 a logical program is described to update an Orders file and produce an Order. When this program is coded in a language such as COBOL or FOCUS, it becomes physical.

Every business system exists to provide information. This information is in the form of reports. (The term *report* includes any human-readable output.) These reports are defined in detail later. If the first cut at this report definition should be done now, it helps the user to define the data needed to meet the objectives and also provides the user views or schemas for canonical synthesis. The data needed to meet the objectives serve as a source to define the entities.

A second approach to identify the entities is to follow the theory described in *Information Engineering* [1], which states that the entities should be identified once the objectives have been listed. The reader may follow either approach. The advantage with the former is that the user does not have to think in terms of entities at first, only in terms of the data needed to meet the objectives.

Table 4.2 lists the data elements required to meet each objective listed in Table 4.1. Table 4.3 lists the logical data entities derived from the data elements listed in Table 4.2. (The reader should ignore the content of each entity in Table 4.3 at this time.)

TABLE 4.2   INFORMATION REQUIRED TO MEET OBJECTIVES

Objective 1

Documentation Identification, Documentation Update Identification, Date Received, Date Processed, Date Filed

Objective 2

Documentation Identification, Date Written Notice to Obsolete Received, Date Obsoleted, Retention Period

Objective 3

Photocopy Documentation Identification, Update Documentation Identification, Archival Document Identification, Date Shipped Off-Site

Objective 4

Photocopy Documentation Identification, Photocopy Update Documentation Identification, Archival Document Identification, Date Filed

Objective 5

Audit Report

Objective 6

Archival Document Identification, Obsoletion Date, Date Obsoleted

TABLE 4.2 INFORMATION REQUIRED TO MEET OBJECTIVES (continued)

Objective 7

Archival Document Identification, Date of Request, Date of Retrieval

Objective 8

User Identification

Objective 9

Documentation Identification, Archival Document Identification, User Identification, Date Charged Out

TABLE 4.3 ENTITY DATA DICTIONARY: NOT NORMALIZED

Documentation

Documentation Identification, Date Document Received, Date Documentation Processed, Date Document Filed, Date Written Notice to Obsolete Received, Date Documentation Obsoleted, Documentation Retention Period (Date Documentation Charged Out, User Identification)

Documentation Update

Documentation Update Identification, Date Update Received, Date Update Processed, Date Update Filed

Photocopy Documentation

Photocopy Documentation Identification, Date Photocopy Processed, Date Photocopy Documentation Shipped Off-Site, Date Photocopy Document Filed

Photocopy Update Documentation

Photocopy Update Documentation Identification, Date Photocopy Update Processed, Date Photocopy Update Shipped Off-Site, Date Photocopy Update Filed

Archival Document

Archival Document Identification, Date Archival Received, Date Archival Processed, Date Archival Shipped Off-Site, Date Archival Document Filed, Date Archival Document Obsoleted (Date Archival Document Requested, Date Archival Document Retrieved, Date Archival Document Charged Out, User Identification, Date Reshipped, Date Refiled)

User

User Identification

Step 3: Prepare the data model.

A data model shows the relationships between entities or records. Unless the data elements need to be identified in the model, it may show only the entity or record associations. (The terms *relationship* and *association* are interchangeable.) Figure 4.2 is a data model showing the associations

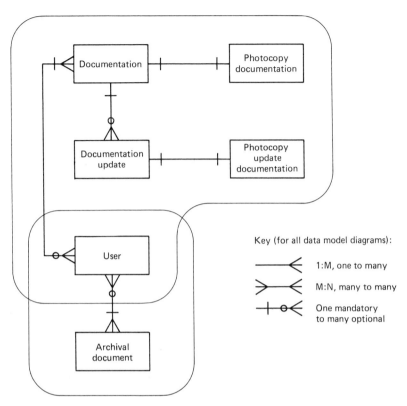

Figure 4.2 Data model showing the relationships between entities in
Table 4.3. Entities are not normalized.

between the entities listed in Table 4.3. The particular associations defined
are numeric relationships, such as 1:1 or many:many, and mandatory or
optional occurrences.

A data model does not show "flow" of data. It shows only static
relationships; hence it can be termed a *static model*. Other techniques use
models which show the flow of data. These are referred to as *dynamic
models*.

Step 4: Expand data on the data dictionary.

Once the logical entities have been identified, they need to be expanded
on the data dictionary. This expansion is done making use of the data
elements identified in Step 2 and the added data provided by the user
based on his knowledge of the application. Some of the data elements
may be described in general terms and expanded again later in Step 7. An
example is Documentation Identification. This will probably become Documentation Number. Table 4.3 lists the entities and their data elements.

Step 5: Partition the data model.

Data models can encompass many functions and can contain entities varying in number from five to many hundred. (Five is used to illustrate a small number. In any actual application, it is very unlikely that the model will contain fewer than twenty entities.) The model should be partitioned so that no partition contains more than fifteen entities unless there is a very good reason to exceed this number. Partitioning is best done based on organizational functions. In our Library System example, the model is partitioned in Figure 4.2 to separate the processing of system documentation from Archival Documents.

Step 6: Normalize the data.

Data normalization of a single record was described in Section 4.3.1. The normalization of a partition of a data model is no different; the problem is only larger. Each entity is normalized separately. (A computerized data dictionary is invaluable at this time.) After normalization is complete, the data dictionary can be used to list the records by data element. This gives the analyst the opportunity to identify duplications of data elements in different records. He can then decide with the user whether the duplications are needed or should be eliminated.

In canonical synthesis, described in Section 4.4, normalization is approached from the viewpoint of multiple schemas (user views of data) imposed one on top of another, like building a brick wall. The basic difference between the two approaches is that the first is entity driven whereas the second is schema driven. This difference should be clearer after the reader has read Section 4.4. Table 4.4 lists the entities and Figure 4.3 shows the data model after normalization.

TABLE 4.4   ENTITY DATA DICTIONARY: NORMALIZED

Documentation

Documentation Identification, Date Document Received, Date Documentation Processed, Date Document Filed, Date Written Notice to Obsolete Received, Date Documentation Obsoleted, Documentation Retention Period

Documentation Charge-out

Documentation Identification, Date Documentation Charged Out, User Identification

Documentation Update

Documentation Update Identification, Date Update Received, Date Update Processed, Date Update Filed

Photocopy Documentation

Photocopy Documentation Identification, Date Photocopy Processed, Date Photocopy Documentation Shipped Off-Site, Date Photocopy Document Filed

TABLE 4.4 ENTITY DATA DICTIONARY: NORMALIZED (continued)

Photocopy Update Documentation

Photocopy Update Documentation Identification, Date Photocopy Update Processed, Date Photocopy Update Shipped Off-Site, Date Photocopy Update Filed

Archival Document

Archival Document Identification, Date Archival Received, Date Archival Processed, Date Archival Shipped Off-Site, Date Archival Document Filed, Date Archival Document Obsoleted

Archival Charge-out

Archival Document Identification, Date Archival Document Requested, Date Archival Document Retrieved, Date Archival Document Charged Out, User Identification, Date Reshipped, Date Refiled

User

User Identification

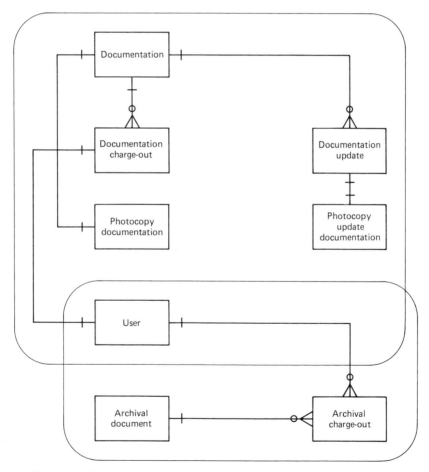

Figure 4.3 Data model showing the relationships between entities in Table 4.4. Entities are normalized.

Step 7: Examine the current data.

No matter how well data have been defined, based on the objectives, it is likely that considerable data have been omitted which are needed to meet both present and future needs. All current registers, logs, files, and so on, whether manual or computerized, are scrutinized and their records with their data elements are entered in the data dictionary, if not already

---

TABLE 4.5 CURRENT DATA IN USE: FOUND IN REGISTERS AND LOGS

Delivery Notice

Document Number, Document Name, Document Volume Number, New/Update, Document Type (Documentation, Archival, etc.), Prepared By, Submitted By, Date Submitted

Daily Register

Document Number, Document Name, Document Volume Number, New/Update, Document Type (Documentation, Archival, etc.), Prepared By, Submitted By, Date Submitted

On-Site Index

Document Number, Document Name, Document Volume Number, Document Type (Documentation, Archival, etc.), Obsoletion Date, Date Filed, Filed By, Type of Access, Term of Loan

Off-Site Index

Document Number, Document Name, Volume Number, Document Type (Documentation, Archival, etc.), Original/Photocopy, Obsoletion Date, Date Obsoleted, Retention Period, Date Destroyed, Destroyed By, Date Filed, Filed By, Off-Site Location

Document Processed Log

Document Number, Document Name, Volume Number, New/Update, Original/Photocopy, Date Processed

Document Shipped Off-Site Register

Document Number, Document Name, Volume Number, New/Update, Original/Photocopy, Date Shipped Off-Site, Date Retrieved from Off-Site

Charge-out Card

Document Number, Document Name, Volume Number, User Identification, Authorized By, Date Charged Out, Date Returned, Date Referenced

History Log

Document Number, Document Name, Volume Number, Date Updated

User Register

User Identification Number, Name, Title, Location, Phone Number

---

recorded there. These data are matched against the entities and the data based on the objectives. The unmatched data are analyzed to determine whether they should be added to the records in the data model or ignored. Table 4.5 lists the Library System's current registers and logs with their data elements.

Step 8: Resolve data conflicts.

The user and the analyst examine the unmatched data and decide whether they should be included or ignored. The highlighted data elements in Table 4.5 are needed and should be added to the data in the data model.

Step 9: Finalize data normalization and complete the data model.

The needed current data are added to the data in the data model and the model is normalized once more. Table 4.6 lists the logical records and their data elements. The reader will note that record and data element names have been shortened. Strictly speaking, every data element should be given a short name which can be used to identify it in the physical files and programs later. Figure 4.4 is the data model illustrating the relationships between the logical records in Table 4.6.

TABLE 4.6 LOGICAL RECORD DATA DICTIONARY: NORMALIZED
_____

Documentation (DOCT)

> DOCT Identification Number, DOCT Name, DOCT Type of Access, DOCT Date Written Notice to Obsolete Received, DOCT Obsoletion Date, DOCT Date Obsoleted, DOCT Retention Period, DOCT Term of Loan

Documentation Volume (DOCVOL)

> DOCT Identification Number, DOCVOL Number, DOCVOL Date Received, DOCVOL Date Processed, DOCVOL Date Filed, DOCVOL Prepared By, DOCVOL Submitted By, DOCVOL Date Destroyed, DOCVOL Destroyed By

Documentation Volume Charge-out (DOCCHOUT)

> DOCT Identification Number, DOCVOL Number, Date DOCCHOUT, USER Identification Number, DOCCHOUT Authorized By, DOCCHOUT Date Charged In

Documentation Volume Reference (DOCREF)

> DOCT Identification Number, DOCVOL Number, Date DOCREF, USER Identification Number, DOCREF Authorized By

TABLE 4.6 LOGICAL RECORD DATA DICTIONARY: NORMALIZED (continued)

Documentation Update (DOCUP)

> <u>DOCT</u> <u>Identification</u> <u>Number</u>, <u>DOCUP</u> <u>Serial</u> <u>Number</u>, DOCUP Prepared By, DOCUP Submitted By, DOCUP Date Received, DOCUP Date Processed, DOCUP Date Filed, DOCUP Filed By

Photocopy Documentation Volume (PHODOCVOL)

> <u>DOCT</u> <u>Identification</u> <u>Number</u>, <u>PHODOCVOL</u> <u>Number</u>, PHODOCVOL Date Processed, PHODOCVOL Date Shipped Off-Site, PHODOCVOL Date Filed, PHODOCVOL Filed By, PHODOCVOL Off-Site Location, PHODOCVOL Date Destroyed, PHODOCVOL Destroyed By

Photocopy Documentation Update (PHODOCUP)

> <u>DOCT</u> <u>Identification</u> <u>Number</u>, <u>PHODOCUP</u> <u>Serial</u> <u>Number</u>, PHODOCUP Date Processed, PHODOCUP Date Shipped Off-Site, PHODOCUP Date Filed, PHODO-CUP Filed By

Archival Document (ARCDOC)

> <u>ARCDOC</u> <u>Name</u>, ARCDOC Term of Loan, ARCDOC Type of Access, ARCDOC Obsoletion Date, ARCDOC Date Obsoleted, ARCDOC Retention Period

Archival Document Copy (ARCDOCCOP)

> <u>ARCDOC</u> <u>Name</u>, <u>ARCDOCCOP</u> <u>Number</u>, ARCDOCCOP Date Received, ARC-DOCCOP Date Processed, ARCDOCCOP Date Shipped Off-Site, ARCDOCCOP Date Filed, ARCDOCCOP Filed By, ARCDOCCOP Off-Site Location, ARC-DOCCOP Date Destroyed, ARCDOCCOP Destroyed By

Archival Document Copy Charge-out (ARCDOCCHOUT)

> <u>ARCDOC</u> <u>Name</u>, <u>ARCDOCCOP</u> <u>Number</u>, <u>Date</u> <u>ARCDOCCHOUT</u>, <u>USER</u> <u>Identification</u> <u>Number</u>, ARCDOCCHOUT Date Requested, ARCDOCCHOUT Authorized By, ARCDOCCOP Date Retrieved, ARCDOCCHOUT Date Charged In, ARCDOCCOP Date Reshipped Off-Site, ARCDOCCOP Date Refiled

Archival Document Copy Reference (ARCDOCREF)

> <u>ARCDOC</u> <u>Name</u>, <u>ARCDOCCOP</u> <u>Number</u>, <u>Date</u> <u>ARCDOCREF</u>, <u>USER</u> <u>Identification</u> <u>Number</u>, ARCDOCREF Authorized By, ARCDOCCOP Date Retrieved, ARCDOCCOP Date Reshipped Off-Site, ARCDOCCOP Date Refiled

User (USER)

> <u>USER</u> <u>Identification</u> <u>Number</u>, USER Name, USER Title, USER Phone Number

Step 10: Cross-check the data model and objectives.

The final data model is cross-checked against the objectives to ensure that the data in the model still satisfy the objectives. It is possible that some iteration of the ten steps can occur, particularly as the user by this time understands his functions and his needs much better than he did when he first stated his objectives.

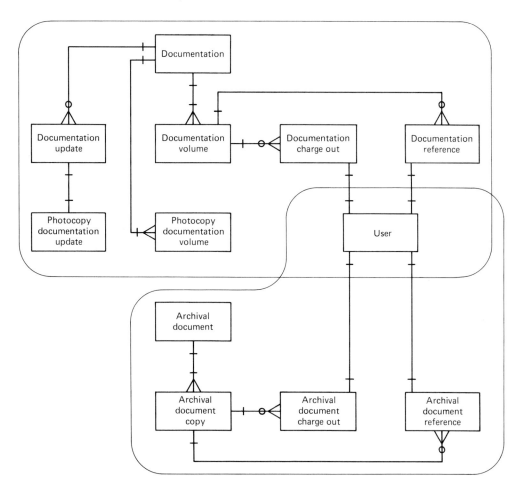

Figure 4.4 Data model showing the relationships between logical records in Table 4.6. Logical records are normalized.

4.4 CANONICAL SYNTHESIS

Canonical synthesis is based on the premise that a canonical schema can be derived from a series of user views of data. Stated another way, it is based on the data requirements of the outputs. It is assumed that a stable data model designed in this way can be updated as the need for additional data requirements arises.

The principle followed in the process is very simple. Take the first user view and normalize it producing a data model. Then take the second user view and superimpose it over the first. Normalize this model. Then take the third and do the same thing until all the user views are incorporated in the model and normalized. Martin describes this process in depth in *Information Engineering* [1] and *Computer Data-Base Organization* [3].

Figure 4.5 illustrates a simple example of canonical synthesis. The notation used here is different from that used in the data models described in Section 4.3 and is in line with Martin's description of the technique.

Each data element is shown as an ellipse. A dependent data element is shown with a single or double arrow pointing to it. A single arrow implies a 1:1 association and a double arrow, a 1:M (many) association. Keys are shaded. A root key (topmost key in the hierarchy) has no single-headed arrows leaving it to another key.

The first user view is a list of documentation destroyed in Date Destroyed sequence and provides the Documentation Number, Name, and

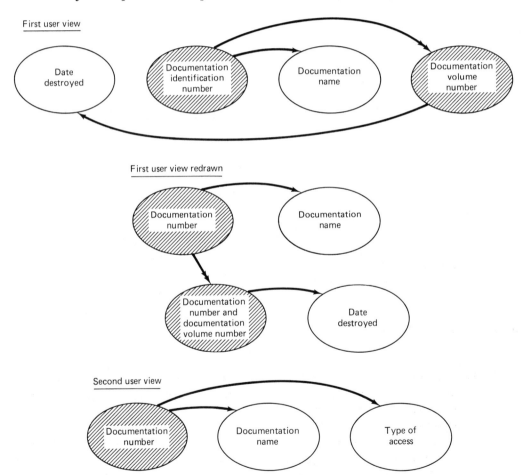

Figure 4.5 Canonical synthesis.

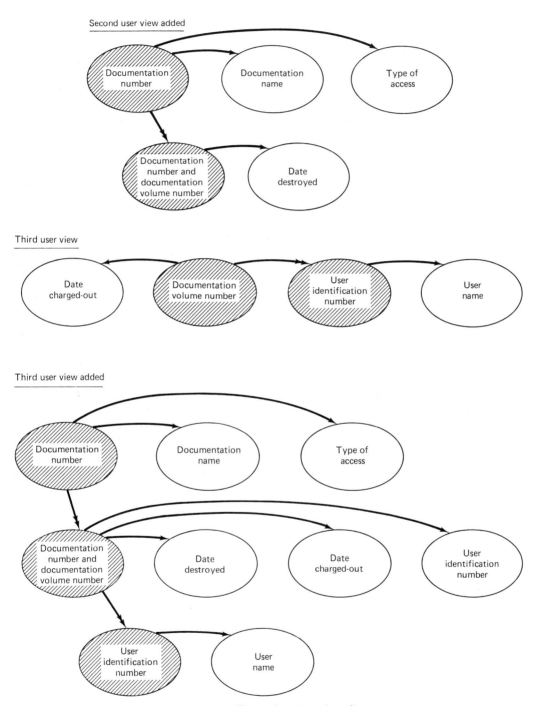

Figure 4.5 *(continued)*

Volume Number. The candidate keys are Documentation Number and Documentation Volume Number. Date Destroyed is dependent on Documentation Volume Number as only a volume can be destroyed. Documentation Name is dependent on Documentation Number, and Documentation Volume has an M:1 dependency on Documentation Number. The model is redrawn showing these relationships. Note that the Volume record has a concatenated key made up of Documentation Number and Documentation Volume Number as the Documentation Volume Number by itself cannot identify the volume.

The second user view is a list of documentation by name and type of access in Documentation Number sequence. Documentation Name and Type of Access are both dependent on Documentation Number. The model is redrawn with the second user view added.

The third user view is a list of documentation charged out in Date Charged Out sequence and provides the User Identification Number and Name. The Date Charged Out is dependent on the Documentation Volume Number. User Identification Number is a new candidate key and has an M:1 dependency on Documentation Volume Number. User Name is dependent on the User Identification Number. The model is again redrawn with the third user view added. Figure 4.6 shows the canonically synthesized data model redrawn using the notation described in Section 4.3. The Documentation Volume record contains the User Identification Number, which is a pointer to the user record.

When canonical synthesis is done manually, it can be both time consuming and frustrating if one is consolidating a large number of possible user views (outputs or schemas). Software is available which has been specifically designed to make this task easier. One such product is called Data Designer [6]. An effective data dictionary or even an unsophisticated sort program could reduce copying, sorting, and the manual errors to make this task easier.

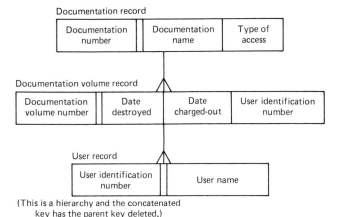

Documentation record

| Documentation number | Documentation name | Type of access |

Documentation volume record

| Documentation volume number | Date destroyed | Date charged-out | User identification number |

User record

| User identification number | User name |

(This is a hierarchy and the concatenated
key has the parent key deleted.)

Figure 4.6 Canonically synthesized data model.

4.5 PROCEDURE FORMATION

In procedure formation, we specify the procedures (processes) on the computer and for the organization's employees to provide the output data needed for planning, decision making, operating, and controlling the business. In other words, we develop procedures to provide the information needed to meet the organization's objectives.

In Chapter 3 we concluded that an information system has five basic components: data input, data input processed, data stored, data output processed, and data output. In information analysis, we described how data input, data stored, and data output are identified. In procedure formation, we describe how the data input and data output processes can be specified. In program specification synthesis, we will discuss the development of standard modules from the input and output processes.

In Chapter 3 we described the processing of input data as file maintenance and the processing of output data as output production. In file maintenance, we add records, delete records, modify records (add, delete, or update data elements), or read (retrieve or access) records. We can also validate records or compute new data element values. In output production, we read records stored in files and produce "reports" on screens, paper, or magnetic storage (disk, tape, etc.). We may also introduce new output records for particular reports. Any physical program may include both file maintenance and output production modules.

Functions performed during file maintenance and output production are called *events.* These events can be divided into five classes:

1. *Basic maintenance:* add, delete, and modify records.
2. *Access:* read or retrieve records.
3. *Validate:* validate records.
4. *Algorithmic:* compute or execute an algorithm to change the value of a data element.
5. *External interfaces:* enter, obtain, exit, print, and so on.

Only add, delete, and modify events can update data in a file. Read or retrieve events can access data in a file but do not change them. So if events were considered to be building blocks, the basic maintenance events would be the foundation, the access events would be the second layer, the validate and algorithmic events would be the third layer, and the external interfaces would be the topmost layer.

Procedure formation has three phases:

1. Procedure discovery
2. Procedure expansion
3. Procedure consolidation

Procedure discovery is the specification phase. Procedure expansion and procedure consolidation are the "rounding-off" phases.

4.5.1 Procedure Discovery

Step 1: Partition the normalized data model into functional groups of logical records (if not already partitioned).

Figure 4.4 is reproduced in Figure 4.7 for the convenience of the reader. The model has two partitions only: one for Documentation and the second for Archival Documents.

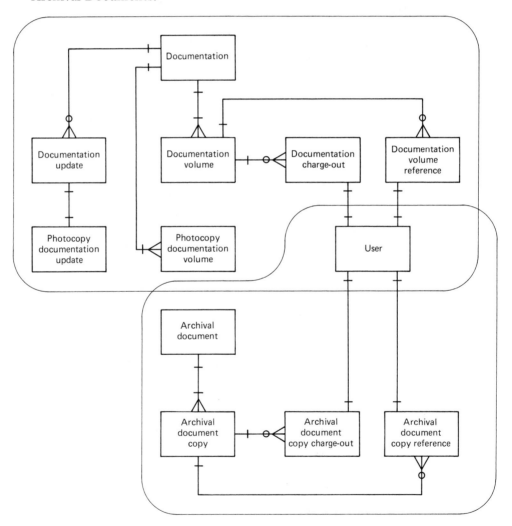

Figure 4.7 Data model showing the relationships between logical records in Table 4.6. Logical records are normalized.

Step 2: For each logical record, identify events for record creation, deletion, and modification. (Access, validation, algorithmic, and external interface events are identified later.)

These events are recorded in an event table. Table 4.7 illustrates part of an event table for the data model in Figure 4.7 and the data dictionary in Table 4.6. The first column in Table 4.7 is the *dynamic*, a term coined by Finkelstein as an event shorthand. It consists of three letters. The first is the event type: A for add, D for delete, and M for modify. The second letter R stands for the record. The third letter is O and stands for occurrence. The second column is the record name. The third column is used only for those data elements which can be modified *after the record is created.* The fourth column is the event number. The fifth column is the event description. The sixth and seventh columns are described in Step 3.

Every record in the data model partition is examined by the user and the events that add, delete, and modify the record defined. When defining the modify events, the user lists only those data elements which may change later or be established after the record is created in the event table. For example, Date Obsoletion Notice Received may become known months or years after the Documentation record is established. On the other hand, the Documentation Name must be defined when the documentation is prepared.

Step 3: Identify the conditions associated with the events.

Every event is associated with at least one and possibly more conditions. These conditions are of two types: The first are the conditions that precede or succeed an event in a procedure. These are "if" conditions. Examples of such conditions are "If Documentation Number is valid," "If End of File," and "If access to Documentation permitted, then . . . ." The second type of condition includes those that trigger a procedure. These are "when" conditions. For example, "When New Document is received" precedes the procedure to set up a new documentation record. An event may be dependent on one or more conditions being satisfied.

When each event is identified, the corresponding conditions are also identified and listed in a condition table. Table 4.8 is the condition table corresponding to the event table, Table 4.7. The condition number and description are also entered in the event table. (The reason for doing this is discussed in Section 4.5.3.)

Step 4: Develop procedures.

Procedures are developed from the data model, the events, and the conditions associated with the events. Martin and Finkelstein approach this step

TABLE 4.7 EVENT TABLE

Dynamic	Record name	Data element	Event number	Event description	Condition number	Condition description
ARO	DOCT		01	Register DOCT	01	When new DOCT received
DRO	DOCT		02	Delete DOCT Record	02	When file is purged
MRO	DOCT	Date Obsolete Notice Received	03	Obsolete DOCT	04	When obsoletion notice received
MRO	DOCT	Obsolete Date	04	Establish obsolete date	04	When obsoletion notice received
MRO	DOCT	Date Obsoleted	05	Record date obsoleted	05	When DOCT is obsoleted
MRO	DOCT	Retention Period	06	Establish retention period	05	When DOCT is obsoleted
ARO	DOCVOL		07	Register DOCVOL	01	When new DOCT is received
DRO	DOCVOL		08	Delete DOCVOL record	02	When file is purged

54

MRO	DOCVOL	Date Filed	09	Register date filed	06	When DOCVOL is filed
MRO	DOCVOL	Date Destroyed	10	Register date destroyed	03	When DOCVOL is destroyed
ARO	DOCCHOUT		11	Charge-out DOCVOL	07	When DOCVOL is borrowed
DRO	DOCCHOUT		12	Delete DOCCHOUT record	02	When file is purged
MRO	DOCCHOUT	Date Charged In	13	Charge-in DOCVOL	08	When DOCVOL is returned
ARO	DOCREF		14	Reference DOCVOL	09	When DOCVOL is referenced
DRO	DOCREF		15	Delete DOCREF record	02	When file is purged
ARO	DOCUP		16	Register DOCUP	10	When DOCUP is received

TABLE 4.8 CONDITION TABLE

Condition number	Condition description	Dynamic	Event number	Event description
01	When new document is received	ARO ARO	01 07	Register DOCT Register DOCVOL
02	When the file is purged	DRO DRO DRO DRO	02 08 12 15	Delete DOCT record Delete DOCVOL record Delete DOCCHOUT record Delete DOCREF record
03	When DOCVOL is destroyed	MRO	10	Register date destroyed
04	When Obsoletion Notice is received	MRO	04	Establish obsoletion date
05	When DOCT is obsoleted	MRO MRO	05 06	Record date obsoleted Establish retention period
06	When DOCVOL is filed	MRO	09	Register date filed
07	When DOCVOL is borrowed	MRO	11	Charge out DOCVOL
08	When DOCVOL is returned	MRO	13	Charge in DOCVOL
09	When DOCVOL is referenced	MRO	14	Reference DOCVOL
10	When DOCUP is received	ARO	16	Register DOCUP

from different viewpoints. My experience with procedure formation has resulted in a variation on Finkelstein's approach. We will examine all three approaches here.

4.5.2 Levels 1, 2, and 3 Procedures (Finkelstein)

This approach is described in detail in *Procedure Formation: Specification (and Design) by Users* [7]. The notation used is illustrated in Figure 4.8. Events are drawn as ellipses, conditions as arrows into and from the events, and the sequence of events follows the conditions clockwise. Note the special notation for "repeat . . . until . . ." and "do . . . while . . ." conditions. (These special conditions are easily identified from the 1:M associations in the data model.) Condition sums are shown with a "+" sign and alternatives with a "/" sign; negative conditions are shown with a bar over them.

In order to isolate procedure derivation from personal knowledge of the organization's business, each condition and its related events in the condition table are drawn as an event diagram showing only the event numbers

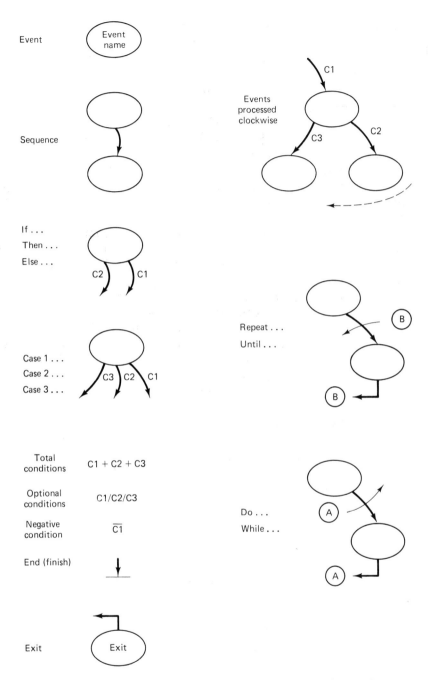

Figure 4.8 Procedure formation notation recommended by Information Methods (USA) Corp.

and condition numbers. If the condition precedes the event, it is drawn above the event, and if it follows the event, below it. Where more than one condition applies, they are linked by "+"s or "/"s as the case dictates. The addition of the event and condition descriptions to these "embryonic" procedures provides level 1 procedures which can be examined to determine if they are meaningful.

Figure 4.9 is a hypothetical embryonic procedure drawn to show how events and combinations can be linked from a condition table. Note how combinations of conditions are illustrated. The procedures shown in Figure 4.10 reflect some of the conditions and events listed in Table 4.8. Condition and event descriptions are added to the diagrams, and the procedures are evaluated. These procedures are termed *level 1 procedures*. Figure 4.11 is Figure 4.10 repeated with the descriptions added.

Access events, validations, and algorithmic computations are added to each level 1 procedure. The resulting diagram is a *level 2 procedure*. Figure 4.12 is procedure P1, "Register new documentation," from Figure 4.11 expanded to level 2.

Interface events are added to the level 2 procedures to produce *level 3 procedures*. Figure 4.13 is the level 3 procedure for procedure P1.

Using the level 1, 2, and 3 procedure approach, you develop only file maintenance procedures, unless output production (excluding input data acceptance reports) is deliberately introduced at level 3. The isolation of file maintenance procedures from output production procedures forces the analyst and the user to develop separate procedures for each output report needed.

Most fourth-generation languages do not require detailed instructions for accessing data from external sources or files, or instructions to print errors. This type of logic is built into the language software. So if the system

Procedure P1

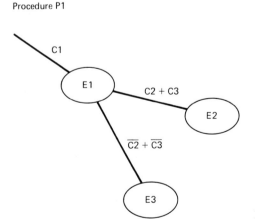

Figure 4.9 Embryonic procedure.

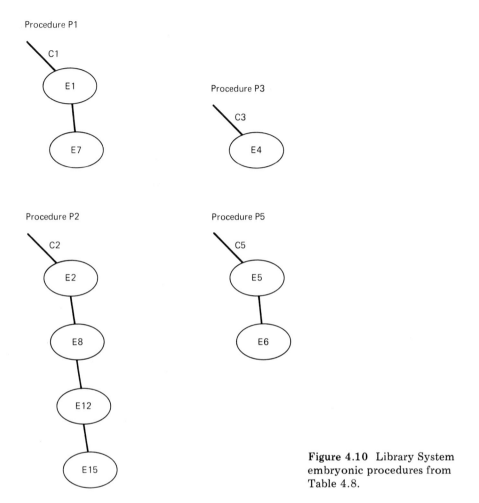

Figure 4.10 Library System
embryonic procedures from
Table 4.8.

is to be built using a language such as FOCUS or RAMIS, the amount of detail required in the event diagrams is considerably reduced.

4.5.3 Flag Conditions (Connor)

In Step 3 we identified two different types of conditions. The first were "if" conditions. The second were "when" conditions. The "when" conditions identify specifically when records are added, deleted, modified, or retrieved. Hence they are referred to as *flag conditions*. Let us look at an example outside the Library System. A customer walks into a bank and opens an account. This sets in progress a chain of events that result in

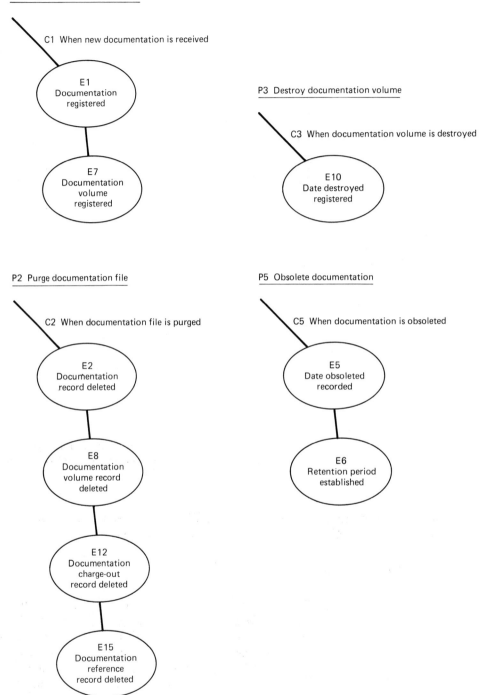

P1 Register new documentation

C1 When new documentation is received

E1
Documentation
registered

E7
Documentation
volume
registered

P3 Destroy documentation volume

C3 When documentation volume is destroyed

E10
Date destroyed
registered

P2 Purge documentation file

C2 When documentation file is purged

E2
Documentation
record deleted

E8
Documentation
volume record
deleted

E12
Documentation
charge-out
record deleted

E15
Documentation
reference
record deleted

P5 Obsolete documentation

C5 When documentation is obsoleted

E5
Date obsoleted
recorded

E6
Retention period
established

Figure 4.11 Library System Level 1 procedures.

P1 Register new documentation

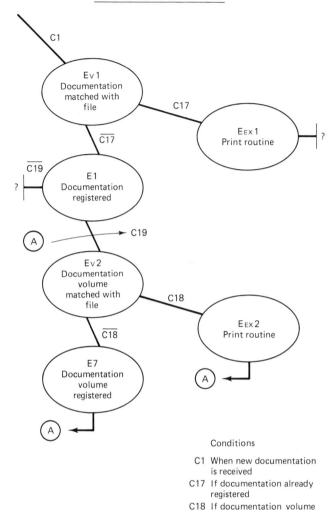

Conditions

C1 When new documentation
     is received
C17 If documentation already
      registered
C18 If documentation volume
      already registered
C19 If more documentation
      volumes to be registered

Figure 4.12 Library System Level
2 procedure. Validation events
incorporated.

several new records being established. Similarly, when he closes an account or dies, he triggers another chain of events which result in some
records being deleted and others being modified. The same thing happens
when he deposits or withdraws money, signs a check, or takes a loan. If
each of these records had been analyzed in terms of the events and conditions which add, delete, modify, or access them, all these "when" conditions would have been identified.

P1 Register new documentation

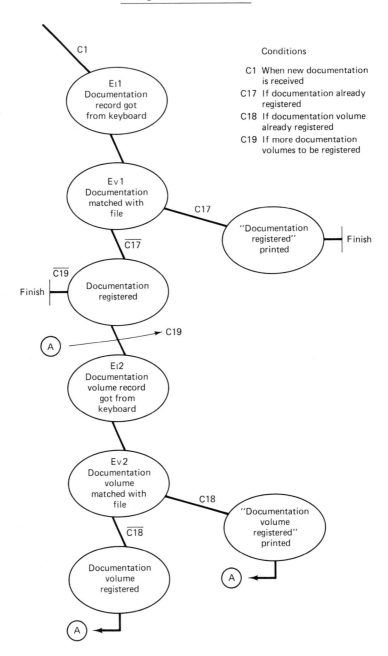

Conditions

C1 When new documentation
     is received
C17 If documentation already
     registered
C18 If documentation volume
     already registered
C19 If more documentation
     volumes to be registered

Figure 4.13 Library System Level 3 procedures. External interfaces incorporated.

Let us return to the program example in Section 3.5. This procedure consists of events that occur "when" *an order for stock is received.* It can be divided into modules that add or modify records, and a module to produce the report. These modules include reads, validates, and computes.

File maintenance

Add Order Header includes validation of Customer Number.	Read Order Header record input. Validate Customer Number. Reject invalid Customer Number. Establish Order Header.
Add Order Item includes Product validation and verification of Stock Quantity.	Read Order Item record input. Validate Product Number. Reject invalid Product Number. Verify Quantity in Stock greater than Quantity ordered. Reject if insufficient Quantity in Stock. Establish Order Item.
Modify Quantity in Stock.	Reduce Quantity in Stock. Repeat Read of Order Item record until no more Order Items.

Output production

Retrieve Customer Name and Customer Address (from Customer Record).
Print Order Header.
Retrieve Product Name and Product Price (from Product record).
Compute Total Product Cost.
Print Order Item.
Compute Order Cost.
Print Order Cost.
Compute Tax 7% of Order Cost.
Print Tax.
Compute Total Order Cost.
Print Total Order Cost.

The first module establishes (adds) the Order Header record. To do this, it validates the Customer Number. The second module establishes (adds) the Order Item. To do this, it validates the Product Number and verifies that the Quantity in Stock is greater than the Quantity Ordered. The third module reduces (modifies) the Quantity in Stock. The fourth module produces a report.

We can conclude from this example that every "when" condition can result in a procedure and that this procedure can be broken down into logical modules which add, delete, or modify records, and modules to produce output reports (or files). Because "when" conditions are so critical, they *must* be included in the event table and the condition table. Should "if" conditions be omitted from these tables, they become evident as soon as the procedures are expanded to level 2 and level 3.

In Step 3 we said that the condition number and description are entered in the event table as well as in the condition table. If we sort the event table by condition, we get the condition table with the records and data elements included, and each "when" condition and its related events becomes a level 1 procedure. Figure 4.11 illustrates these "when" conditions and their level 1 procedures for the Library System. Each of these level 1 procedures can now be expanded to level 2 and level 3, just as we did in Section 4.5.2.

4.5.4 LAMs and DADs (Martin)

LAM stands for *logical access map* and DAD stands for *data-base action diagram*. Every procedure has an access path through a data model. Martin states in *LAMs and DADs* [8] that the access path through the data model must be drawn before the procedure is developed. This access path is a LAM. Once the path is identified, the procedure is described using a DAD. Later, the LAMs are used in data use analysis to determine the specifications of the physical data base or file.

Each LAM is derived from the "user views" or outputs required from the system being designed. The "user view" or output could be a file update or be human readable. Figure 4.14 is a LAM for an "Accept orders for stock" procedure. This procedure is the file maintenance half of the program in Section 3.5. The records accessed in the data base are Customer, Order Header, Product, and Order Item in that sequence. Table 4.9 is the data dictionary for these records.

The DAD describing this procedure is shown in Figure 4.15. The reader will note that Martin's notation used to draw the DAD is completely different from Finkelstein's. It is based on a system of brackets. Figure 4.16 illustrates how the brackets are drawn and how the events and conditions relate to the brackets. Events are *only* those actions which add, delete, modify, or read records. Validations and computations are *not* considered events. Each event is drawn as a lozenge below its related record in the data base. In Figure 4.15, the LAM corresponding to the DAD is drawn vertically beside it.

Aside from the procedure notation, the basic difference between the Martin and Finkelstein approaches is whether the data access path should be drawn before or after the procedure is described. Finkelstein's approach using embryonic procedures which are directly extracted from the condition table makes procedure definition almost an automatic exercise. My approach, based on the "when" conditions, can also be considered an auto-

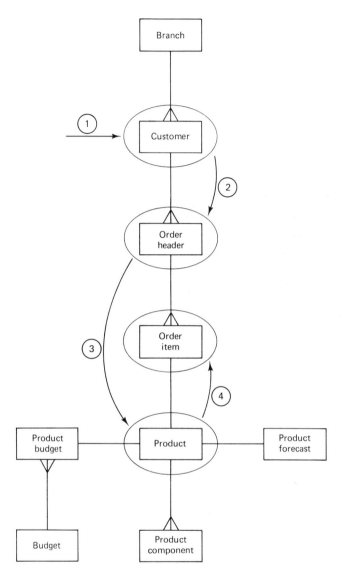

Figure 4.14 LAM (Logical Access Map) of the data model for "Accent Order for Stock" procedure.

TABLE 4.9 DATA DICTIONARY FOR ORDERS DATA MODEL

Customer (Customer Number, Customer Name, Customer Address)
Order Header (Order Number, Customer Number)
Product (Product Number, Product Name, Product Price, Quantity in Stock)
Order Item [Line Item in the order] (Order Number, Item Number, Product Number, Quantity Ordered)

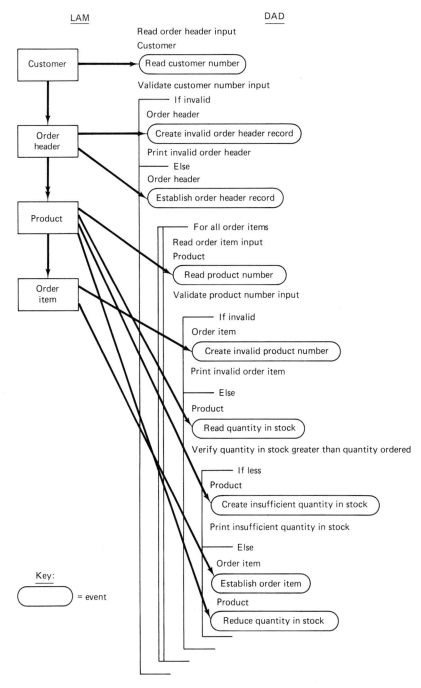

Figure 4.15 DAD (Database Action Diagram) of the data model for "Accent Order for Stock" procedure.

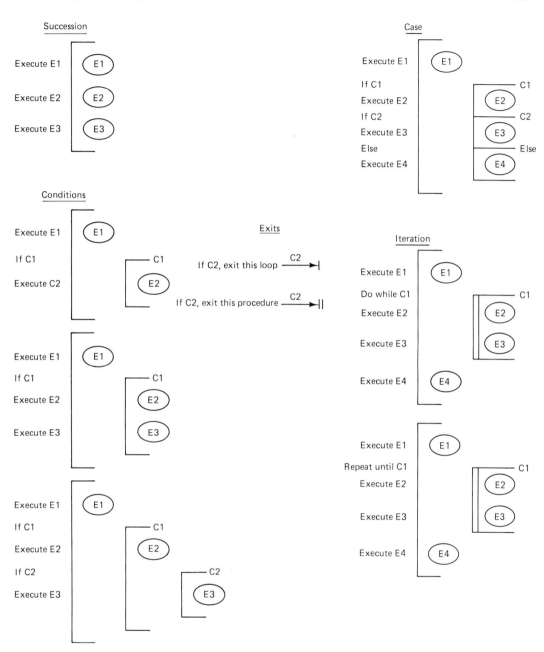

Figure 4.16 LAM notation.

matic exercise. Both Finkelstein's and my approaches emphasize file maintenance. Martin's approach, in which the access path is traced through the data model before the procedure is defined, ensures that the model can produce the outputs. Hence it is directed at output production. LAMs and DADs are not produced automatically and require some analytical thinking.

4.5.5 Procedure Expansion

In this phase, each procedure is checked against the data model to ensure that the data model can satisfy the procedures and that no critical procedure has been omitted. Next, the procedures are checked against the objectives. These checks could result in the procedures being expanded.

4.5.6 Procedure Consolidation

In this phase, the procedures are formally documented either as module or program specifications, or as manual procedures. Similar procedures from other data models may be grouped together. Current procedures should be cross-checked against the new procedures. Current organizational boundaries may be affected and require restructuring.

A final check against the data model should be made to ensure that the data model still satisfies any changes made to the procedures. This final check is done during data use analysis when each procedure is traced through the data model.

4.6 PROGRAM SPECIFICATION SYNTHESIS

In "English," *program specification synthesis* translates into developing a data dictionary of modules which can be accessed by any program that requires them. In *Information Engineering* [1], this process is described in detail so that every data element in every record that can be added, deleted, modified, or retrieved can be automatically called by a program. The approach described here is restricted to standard modules at the record level.

4.6.1 Associations between Records

We know already that associations between records can be 1:1, 1:M (many), or M:N (many:many). Let us look at an example: Figure 4.17 is a data model with four records. These are Archival Document, Archival Document

Copy, Archival Document Charge-out, and User. The first three form a hierarchy and are linked by their keys. The link between Archival Document Charge-out and User is not part of a hierarchy. The link is through the data element User Identification Number.

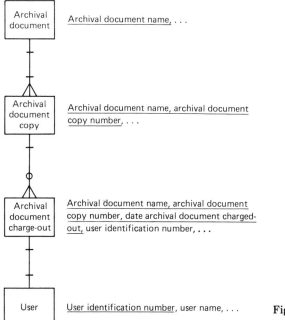

| Archival document | Archival document name, . . . |

| Archival document copy | Archival document name, archival document copy number, . . . |

| Archival document charge-out | Archival document name, archival document copy number, date archival document charged-out, user identification number, . . . |

| User | User identification number, user name, . . . |

Figure 4.17 Associations between records.

A data processing organization could have access to a relational data base, to a hierarchical or CODASYL data base, or could be working with procedural languages such as COBOL or PL/1. If it uses a fourth-generation language such as FOCUS, the language would probably have a data base built into it which could be relational, CODASYL, or hierarchical.

If your programs are accessing a relational data base, no additional associations need be established. The relational algebra or calculus provides the links. If you are working with a CODASYL or hierarchical data base, links are provided through "sets" or the data-base hierarchy. Where there is no hierarchical or set link, as between Archival Document Charge-out and User, a virtual link must be defined either in the data base or in the program. Where no data base is being used, the program must "call" each new record by identifying the key involved. Including these associations as part of the module specifications in the data dictionary provides the programmer with a reminder that a link is needed.

4.6.2 Secondary Records

Secondary records are records that can be derived from the data in the
data model but which are required consistently. These records, if stored,
save processing time. The most common example of a secondary record
is a Month-to-Date Total. These records should be identified, added to
the data model and the data dictionary, and clearly identified as secondary
records. This means that if the objectives change or there is a need to update the data model for any reason, the original, normalized data model is
updated first and the secondary records updated later.

Merely adding the secondary records to the data model is not enough.
These additional records must also be put onto a separate event table and
the add, delete, modify, and retrieve events, and related "when" conditions
identified. This ensures that file maintenance modules are developed for
these secondary records.

4.6.3 Output Specification

The definition of outputs and their record content serves two purposes:
(1) to help identify secondary records and (2) to develop standard modules
for output production. In Step 2 of information analysis, we made a first
attempt at identifying the outputs. If we had used canonical synthesis or
prepared LAMs and DADs, it is likely that we would already have the outputs defined in terms of their record content. If we do not yet have the
record content of the outputs defined, they should be done now. On the
other hand, the user may not be able to define all the outputs he requires
now or may wish to leave the door open to define more, as and when the
need arises. This is not a problem, as the data model should be able to satisfy
the additional output requirements.

4.6.4 Standard Modules

A *standard module* is a module developed in line with a standard specification. We stated in Section 3.4 that there are five basic types of modules
which should meet any file update or output requirement. These are add
record, delete record, modify (add, delete, or change the value of a data element) record, retrieve (access) record, and produce output. We can establish specifications for each type and include in these specifications provision
for validations and computations. In this way, we ensure consistency in our

module and program structure. Further, it becomes a very simple task to develop any of these modules if we store the basic structure in a dictionary and call it up when a module is to be developed.

To illustrate standard modules, let us look at some examples based on the following records:

- Product (<u>Product</u> <u>Number</u>, Product Name, Product Price, Quantity in Stock)

- Order Item (<u>Order</u> <u>Number</u>, <u>Item</u> <u>Number</u>, Product Number, Quantity Ordered)

Example 1   Add Product Record

Read Product record input.
Match Product Number (key) with Product Number in file.
   If matched, reject Product record input.
      Print rejected Product record.
   If not matched, establish Product record in file.
      Add Product Name, Product Price, Quantity in Stock.
Repeat until no more Product records input.

Example 2   Add Order Item Record

Read Order Item record input.
Match Order Number and Order Item Number (key) with Order Number and Order Item Number in file.
   If matched, reject Order Item record.
      Print rejected Order Item record.
   If not matched, validate Product Number.
      Match Product Number with Product Number in Product file.
         If not matched, reject Order Item record.
            Print rejected Order Item record.
         If matched, verify Quantity in Stock greater than Quantity Ordered.
            Compute Quantity in Stock from Product file greater than Quantity Ordered.
               If Quantity in Stock less than Quantity Ordered, reject Order Item record.
                  Print rejected Order Item record.
               If Quantity in Stock greater than Quantity Ordered, establish Order Item record.
                  Add Product Number, Quantity Ordered.
Repeat until no more Order Item records input.

In this example, we added a validation and a computation to the basic module.

Example 3 Modify Product Record

> Read Product record input.
> Match Product Number (key) with Product Number in file.
>> If not matched, reject Product record input.
>>> Print rejected Product record.
>> If matched, modify Product record in file.
>>> Compute Quantity in Stock = Quantity in Stock minus Quantity Ordered from Order Item record.
>>> Update Quantity in Stock.
> Repeat until no more Product records input.

In this example, we added a computation to the basic module.

The standard add, delete, and modify modules need to be coded in the particular programming language to be used. If the same programming language is used all the time, the basic modules can be coded in that language and stored in the dictionary. Modules to produce output are more difficult to standardize because they can be expected to execute all manner of instructions. The simplest and most effective way to produce outputs is to use a fourth-generation query language.

4.6.5 Master Index Hierarchies

If we establish add, delete, modify, and retrieve modules for every record in the data model, we can access these modules directly if we are using an on-line system or we can combine them in programs if we are using a batch

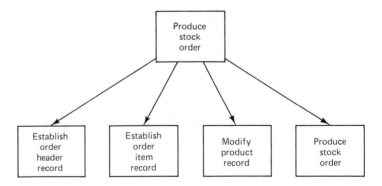

Figure 4.18 "Produce Stock Order" procedure and related modules in a hierarchy.

system. All that we need to know is which modules are needed in any procedure. We already know this because we know the basic events that make up the procedure and each of these events is now a separate module. Figure 4.18 illustrates a procedure and its modules as a hierarchy. This hierarchy is flat, as it has only two levels. In practice, we might wish to increase these levels for convenience. For example, all four basic modules for one record may be combined in a single program. When this program is called by the procedure, only the necessary modules will be executed. The hierarchies may be further expanded by building menus which take you from a high level to the module level. Figure 4.19 illustrates this type of hierarchy.

Before we leave the subject of information engineering, I would like to remind the reader that he can practice the theories of information engineering by expanding on some of the examples covered in the text. Try to develop the normalized data model for the Library System on your own. Expand the event and condition tables. Develop standard modules and establish detailed hierarchies for them which will enable you to provide any information the user may require.

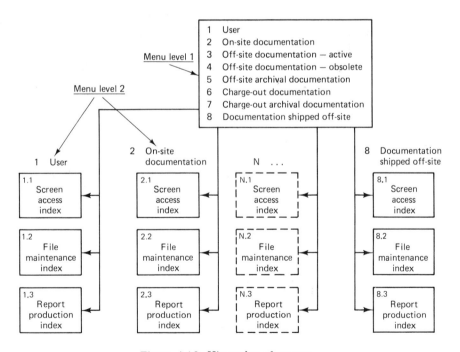

Figure 4.19 Hierarchy of menus.

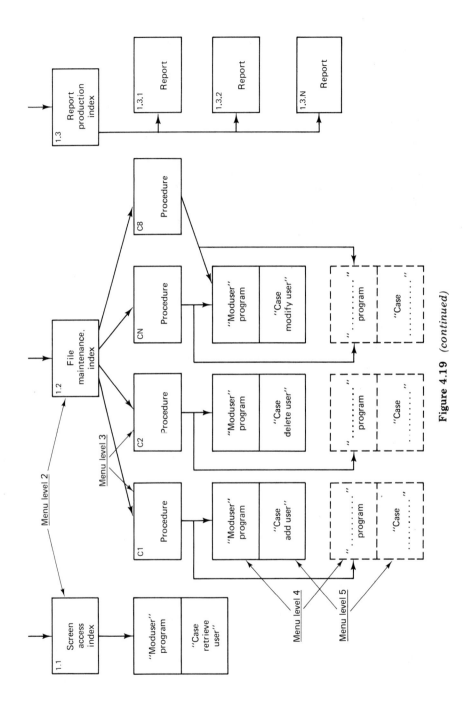

Figure 4.19 *(continued)*

4.7 ADVANTAGES AND DISADVANTAGES
OF INFORMATION ENGINEERING

Information engineering embraces a wide variety of subjects and these subjects are addressed differently by Martin and Finkelstein. For example, Martin advocates canonical synthesis, whereas Finkelstein does not. Both viewpoints have advantages and disadvantages. Rather than enter into an in-depth analysis of the two approaches, we will look only at the overall picture in terms of advantages and disadvantages.

Advantages

1. Systems are designed based on data and data relationships which have been derived from management's objectives and current data in use. These systems are not based on the flow of data. Since data flow is not required, this results in considerable time savings and permits designers (users and analysts) to concentrate their attention on the items that are most critical (i.e., the data).

2. All the system's data have been normalized. Data normalization ensures data stability and either reduces or eliminates data redundancy.

3. All redundant data have been eliminated from the files and we are left with primary and secondary records which are clearly identified in the data dictionary.

4. File maintenance procedures are developed based on events that add, delete, modify, and retrieve data. Output procedures are separated from the maintenance procedures.

5. Stable, logical data bases or files are obtained which easily convert to physical data bases or files. These logical data bases have been produced primarily by the users and, as a result, the users completely understand and relate to them.

Disadvantages

1. Information engineering is not suited to the development of systems with a strong time dimension such as an elevator system or a missile guidance system. This is because the system is designed on the basis of a static data model which emphasizes data storage and data update. In dynamic systems, the emphasis is on time-related change in conditions and processes, while the storage of data is only a secondary consideration.

REFERENCES

1. James Martin and Clive Finkelstein, *Information Engineering*, Savant Research Studies, 2 New Street, Carnforth, Lancashire, LA5 9BX, England, 1981.

2. Clive Finkelstein, six articles on information engineering, *Computerworld*, May 11 to June 15, 1981.

3. James Martin, *Computer Data-Base Organization*, 2nd ed., Prentice-Hall, Inc., Englewood Cliffs, NJ, 1977.

4. E. F. Codd, "Further Normalization of the Data Base Relational Model," in *Data Base Systems*, edited by Randall Rustin, © 1972, pp. 66–98. Adapted by permission of Prentice-Hall, Inc., Englewood Cliffs, NJ.

5. Jean-Dominique Warnier, *Logical Construction of Systems*, Van Nostrand Reinhold Company, Inc., New York, 1981.

6. Data Designer, sold by Data Base Design Inc., 3001 South State Road, 4th Floor, Ann Arbor, MI 48104.

7. Robert M. Rollason and Clive Finkelstein, *Procedure Formation: Specification (and Design) by Users*, Information Engineering Series, Information Engineering (Aust) Pty. Ltd., Highland Centre, 7-9 Merriwa Street, Gordon, New South Wales 2072, Australia.

8. James Martin, *LAMs and DADs*, Savant Research Studies, 2 New Street, Carnforth, Lancashire LA5 9BX, England, 1982.

Structured Analysis
and Design

5.1 WHAT ARE STRUCTURED ANALYSIS AND DESIGN?

5.1.1 Structured Analysis Defined

In *Structured Analysis and System Specification* [1], Tom DeMarco defines *structured analysis* as the use of

- Data flow diagrams
- Data dictionary
- Structured English
- Decision tables
- Decision trees

to build a target document which is the structured specification. These tools meet the two basic needs of effective systems design. They provide a communications mechanism between the analysts and the users, and a precise means of recording the specification so that the design can be translated into computer code and implemented.

What are these tools?

A *data flow diagram* is a charting tool which traces a network of data flows through a system and provides information at varying levels of detail. This enables the system requirement to be partitioned, analyzed, and specified in manageable pieces.

The *data dictionary* provides a means of tracking interfaces in the data flow diagrams.

Structured English, *decision tables*, and *decision trees* describe the flow of process logic more effectively than narrative English.

These tools are explained in detail later in this chapter.

5.1.2 Structured Design Defined

In *Structured Design* [2], Yourdon and Constantine define *structured design* as "the art of designing the components of a system and the interrelationships between these components in the best possible way." They also define it as "the process of deciding which components interconnected in which way will solve some well specified problem." Both these definitions are very general and could be applied to any effective system design technique. A more precise definition would be to state that "structured design is a strategy used to convert the target document obtained from structured analysis into an implementable computer system using the principles and tools of structured design." These include

- Structure charts
- Coupling
- Cohesion
- Transform analysis
- Transaction analysis
- Packaging of modules

Structure charts are hierarchical charts similar to organization charts which relate the flow of data and of control between logical or physical modules.

Coupling and *cohesion* describe the level of dependency between modules.

Transform and *transaction analysis* are tools for analyzing series of processes and optional processes (transactions).

Packaging of modules is the combining of logical module processes to provide physical modules.

These tools are also explained in detail later in this chapter.

5.2 STRUCTURED ANALYSIS

5.2.1 Tools of Structured Analysis

Before we examine the tools of structured analysis in depth, let us look at a simple illustration of their use. Figure 5.1 is a data flow diagram of the Library System documentation update function. Each data flow is illustrated by a line or vector into or from a bubble. Each bubble represents a process, and each file, log, or register is represented by a straight line.

Describing this data flow diagram in narrative form, we have the Documentation-Update submitted to the library accompanied by a Delivery-

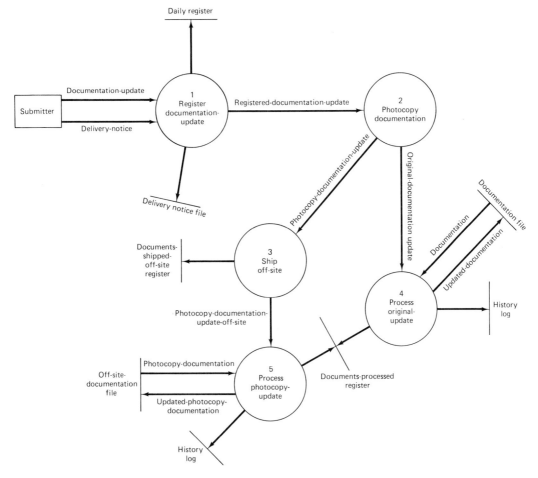

Figure 5.1 Data flow diagram of the documentation update function.

Notice. The Documentation-Update is checked for completeness and is entered in the Daily Register. The Delivery-Notice is filed in the Delivery-Notice File. The registered Documentation-Update is photocopied.

The Original-Documentation-Update is entered in the On-Site History Log attached to the original Documentation. The Documentation-Update is inserted in the original Documentation and the Documentation is filed.

The Photocopy-Documentation-Update is entered in the Documents-Shipped-Off-Site Register and shipped off-site, where it is entered in the Off-Site-History Log attached to the Off-Site-Documentation. The Photocopy-Update is inserted in the Off-Site-Documentation, which is filed. Both the original and the photocopy are entered in the Documents-Processed Log.

Let us now look at an example of a data dictionary entry for the Documentation-Update data flow into bubble 1. It consists of

> Documentation-Identification-Number + Documentation-Update-Serial-Number + Update-Prepared-By + Update-Submitted-By + Update-Date-Received + Update-Date-Processed + Update-Date-Filed + Update-Filed-By

This entry completely describes Documentation-Update.

Bubble 1 in Figure 5.1 could be described in structured English as follows:

> Check Delivery-Notice for completeness.
>> If incomplete, return Delivery-Notice and Documentation-Update to submitter.
>> Else check Documentation-Update for completeness.
>>> If incomplete, return Delivery-Notice and Documentation-Update to Submitter.
>>> Else Enter Update-Documentation in Daily Register.
>>>> File Delivery-Notice.

This simple example should give the reader an introduction to the tools used in structured analysis. We now move on to look at each of them in depth.

5.2.1.1 Data flow diagram. What is a data flow diagram? We defined a data flow diagram in Section 5.1.1. Tom DeMarco defines it [1] as follows:

> A data flow diagram is a network representation of a system. The system may be automated, manual or mixed. The data flow diagram portrays the system in terms of its component pieces, with all interfaces among the components indicated.

Data flow composition. Data flow diagrams are composed of four basic elements:

1. Data flows, represented by named lines or vectors
2. Processes, represented by circles or bubbles
3. Files, represented by straight lines
4. Data sources or sinks, represented by boxes

Data Flows: In Figure 5.1, Documentation-Update, Delivery-Notice, and Registered-Documentation-Update are data flows. Documentation-Update and Registered-Documentation-Update have the same content, but are given different names because a significant action has been taken that affects Documentation-Update. In essence, a data flow is a pipeline which conveys packets of information that are related. If information is not related, separate data flows are drawn as shown by Delivery-Notice and Documentation-Update. The Delivery-Notice is not part of the Documentation-Update.

Data flows do not represent controls, such as "Read-next-record," or process activators, such as "Day-of-week." Controls and process activators are considered only during system design and are not taken into account during analysis.

Data flow names are hyphenated. No two data flows have the same name, as illustrated by Documentation-Update and Registered-Documentation-Update. Names are chosen based on content and action taken on the data flow.

Processes: A process transforms incoming data flows into outgoing data flows. The process name is written as an action verb followed by a noun: for example, Register Documentation-Update.

Files: A file is a temporary data storage. It represents any form of storage and includes an in-box, a disk file, a tape file, and a data-base management system. During analysis, the emphasis is on the data stored and not on the storage medium.

Data flows linking files to processes need not be named. Arrows drawn on the data flows indicate the net flow of data only. For example, a file update implies an initial file access. An analyst may be tempted to draw a double-headed arrow to show this flow. This would be incorrect. The correct notation is a single arrow pointing to the file, indicating the net change to the file.

Source or Sink: A source or sink is an individual or organizational unit outside the boundary of the system that interfaces with the system.

Leveled data flow diagrams.   One of the advantages of a data flow diagram is that it clearly and graphically represents a flow of data through a system. The case study Library System, which is not a large system, involves more than a hundred processes. If this system were charted using a data flow diagram, the chart would cover a large wall area. Such a chart is difficult to absorb and keep up to date. To overcome this problem, we use the concept of leveled data flow diagrams. Figure 5.2 illustrates this concept.

The highest level is drawn as a large circle and represents the entire system. It is called the *context diagram*. The next level shows the major processes in the system. This level is termed the *zero level*. Each of these processes can be exploded to a further level of detail termed *level 1*. This level can be exploded in turn until the lowest level, called a *functional primitive bubble*, is reached. (The reader should note that primitives can occur at any level,

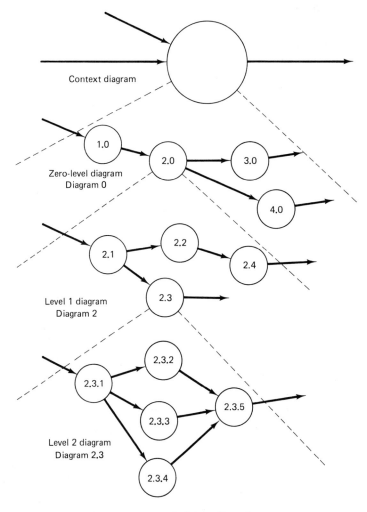

Figure 5.2 Leveled data flow diagram.

including the zero level.) A *primitive* is a process which generally executes a single function and can be described in less than a page of structured English. When the lowest level consists only of primitives, the leveling is complete.

Each diagram that is drawn is given a number. Referring to Figure 5.2, each level shown is numbered in terms of its parent. For example, the level 1 diagram shown is diagram 2, as it charts the children of bubble 2.0.

Principle of data conservation. The principle of data conservation states: A process must be able to build its outputs using only the information in data flows explicitly shown flowing into it, plus constant information [1]. In other words, a process cannot create data by itself, nor can it lose them. The same principle applies to leveling. A data flow at a higher level can include several data flows at a lower level. This is recorded in the data dictionary entry for the higher-level data flow. The addition of data flows at the lower levels, which have not been included in the higher level, are not permitted.

Iteration. The drawing of data flows is a highly iterative process. This is because you learn more and more about the system as you proceed and any change made at a lower level affects at least the level above it. It is suggested that the reader refrain from "artwork" until he is reasonably confident that the diagram will not suffer major changes.

5.2.1.2 Data dictionary. The purpose served by the data dictionary during structured analysis is to maintain definitions of

- Data flows
- Components of data flows
- Data elements
- Files
- Processes

During analysis, we are not concerned about related information, such as frequencies, volumes, security considerations, and so on. This information is needed and is acquired only during system design.

The dictionary may be maintained on a computerized package or manually using index cards, or by a combination of both. It really does not matter except in terms of the manual work involved.

Data dictionary notation. The basic information included in each data flow or file entry is

- Name
- Aliases (if any)

- Composition
- Notes (if any)

The basic information included in each process (primitive) entry is

- Process name
- Process number
- Process description

The data flow name, as already described, identifies the content of the data flow and the action taken on it. The alias is any other name by which the data flow may be known. If an alias is used, it must be defined separately in the dictionary.

The composition of a data flow can be quite complex. The conventions used are illustrated below by some simple examples. The conventions used are

=   means *is equivalent to.*

+   means *and.*

[ ] means *either-or* (i.e., select one of the options enclosed in the brackets).

{ } means *iterations* of the components enclosed.

( ) means that the enclosed component is *optional.*

Example 1

Documentation-Update =
Documentation-Identification-Number + Documentation-Update-Serial-Number + Update-Prepared-By + Update-Submitted-By + Update-Date-Received + Update-Date-Processed + Update-Date-Filed + Update-Filed-By

This example illustrates the And and the Equivalent to notations.

Example 2

Employee-Identification =
[Employee-Identification-Number/Employee-Name]

This example illustrates the options available.

Example 3

History-Log =
Documentation-Number + {Documentation-Update}

This example illustrates iterations: in this case, Documentation-Update entries in the History-Log.

Example 4

Employee-Identification =
Employee-Identification-Number + Employee-Name + (Employee-Alias)

This example illustrates the optional component. Here, Employee-Alias is optional.

Logical and physical file descriptions can include data structure diagrams (data models) showing associations or relationships between records. (This subject has been discussed in depth in Chapter 4.) Where complex files occur, it is sufficient to cross-reference the file to the appropriate file description and structure elsewhere in the data dictionary.

The Notes require no special explanation; neither do the process name and number. The process description can be in structured English, decision tables, or decision trees. We discuss minispecifications using structured English in the next section. Decision tables and decision trees are not discussed here. Should the reader require more information on these topics, he should refer to DeMarco's *Structured Analysis and System Specification* [1].

5.2.1.3 Minispecifications using structured English. A minispecification describes the logic involved in the functional primitive. This is done using Bohm and Jacopini's (see Myers [3]) basic constructs (i.e., sequence, selection, and iteration). Sequence implies that one action follows another as soon as the first is completed. Selection implies a choice of actions. Iteration implies that the same action is repeated until a condition is satisfied or while a condition exists. These constructs are illustrated using the following examples:

Example 1   Add Product Record

Read Product record input.
Match Product Number (key) with Product Number in file.
    If matched, reject Product record input.
        Print rejected Product record.
    If not matched, establish Product record in file.
        Add Product-Name, Product-Price, Quantity-in-Stock.

This example illustrates sequence and selection.

Example 2   Add Order Item Record

Read Order-Item record input.
Match Order-Number and Order-Item-Number (keys) with Order-Number and Order-Item-Number in file.
    If matched, reject Order-Item record.
        Print rejected Order-Item record.
    If not matched, validate Product-Number.
        Match Product-Number with Product-Number in Product file.

If not matched, reject Order-Item record.
    Print rejected Order-Item record.
If matched, verify Quantity-in-Stock greater than Quantity-Ordered.
    Compute Quantity-in-Stock from Product file greater than Quantity-Ordered.
        If Quantity-in-Stock less than Quantity-Ordered reject Order-Item record.
           Print rejected Order-Item record.
        If Quantity-in-Stock greater than Quantity-Ordered establish Order-Item record.
           Add Product-Number, Quantity-Ordered.
Repeat until no more Order-Item records input.

This example illustrates sequence, selection, and iteration.

Example 3   Update Quantity in Stock

Read Product record input.
Match Product-Number (key) with Product-Number in file.
    If not matched, reject Product record input.
        Print rejected Product record.
    If matched, modify Product record in file.
        Compute Quantity-in-Stock = Quantity-in-Stock minus Quantity-Ordered from Order-Item record.
        Update Quantity-in-Stock.
Repeat until no more Product records input.

This example also illustrates sequence, selection, and iteration. (The reader should recognize these modules from Section 4.6.3.)

5.2.2 Steps in Structured Analysis

We have described the tools of structured analysis. Next we apply them. Figure 5.3 is a data flow diagram illustrating the seven steps involved.

5.2.2.1 Studying the current physical environment.   In this step (Step 1) we record the flow of information through the current system. We make no attempt to distinguish between logical and physical structures. The outputs from this step are data flow diagrams of the current system with all data flows and files recorded in the data dictionary. The data flow diagram should clearly indicate the context or scope of the system and all known external interfaces.

Figure 5.4 is the level 0 diagram for the Library System. It contains eleven bubbles and lists all the data flows and files. The reader should compare this diagram and the level 1 diagrams drawn in Figures 5.5 to 5.7 with the conventional system diagrams drawn in Chapter 2.

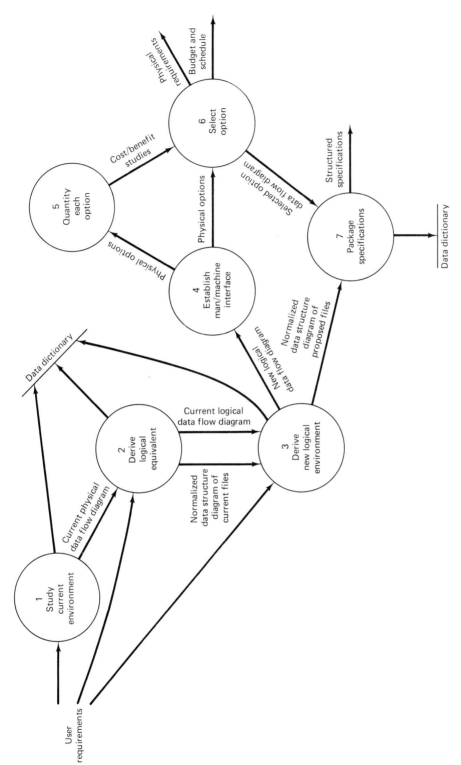

Figure 5.3 Data flow diagram showing the flow of information during structured analysis.

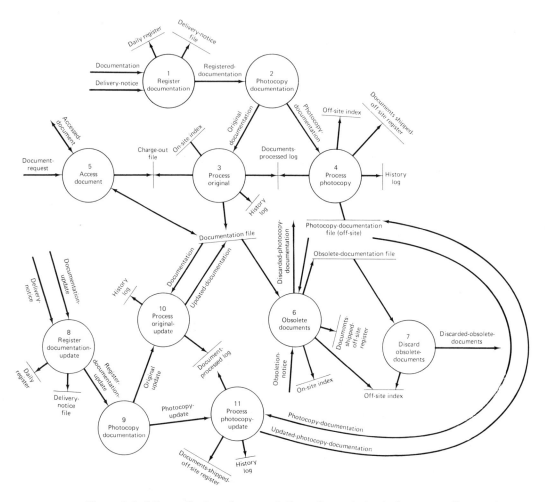

Figure 5.4 Library System documentation: Current physical system—diagram 0.

Table 5.1 is a partial data dictionary for the current system. It lists only the files and registers. It does not list the data flows. The reader may find it worthwhile and interesting to complete the remaining data flow diagrams and to add the data flows to the data dictionary for the Library System.

5.2.2.2 Deriving the logical equivalent of the current environment. In this step (Step 2) we strip away all the physical features of the system. For example, a form in Step 1 may contain one or more records. In this step, we eliminate the form and take into account only the record data.

A second activity, which is often not understood and so not done, or left by the systems analysts to the data administration staff to be done as they see fit, is the normalization of current files. This must be done to eliminate all the uncontrolled data redundancies in these files and to build a stable data model which can be expanded in terms of the user's new requirements in Step 3 (Section 5.2.2.3). DeMarco's approach to normalization is based on accesses to each current file and the identification of the specific data required during each access. Rather than introduce a new approach to normalization over and above the two approaches discussed in Chapter 4, the reader can apply either the basic normalization technique or canonical synthesis. If canonical synthesis is used, each access can be treated as a separate user view or schema.

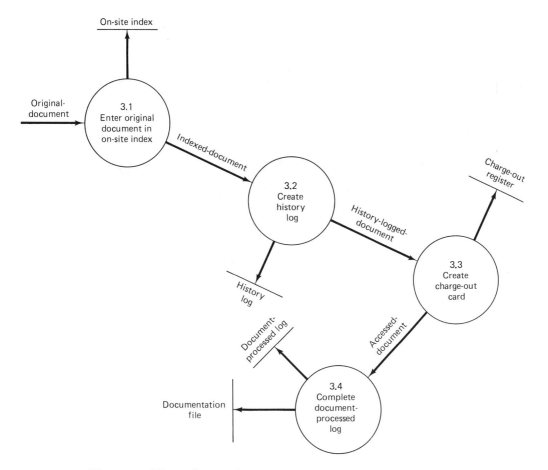

Figure 5.5 Library System documentation: Current physical system—diagram 3.

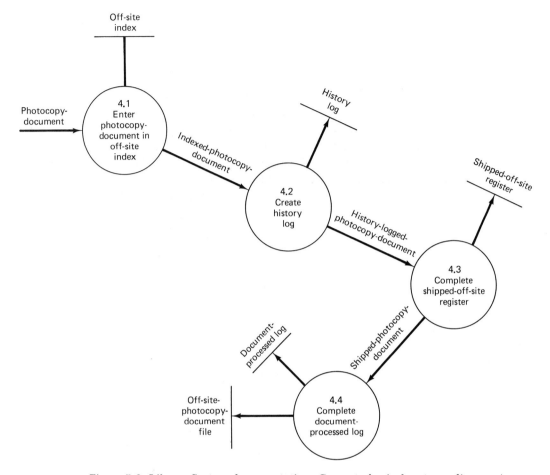

Figure 5.6 Library System documentation: Current physical system—diagram 4.

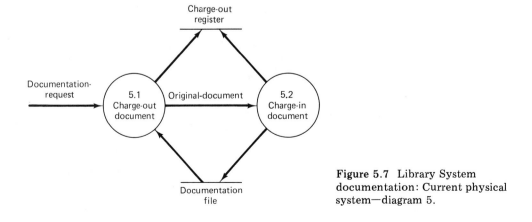

Figure 5.7 Library System documentation: Current physical system—diagram 5.

TABLE 5.1 CURRENT DATA IN USE: FOUND IN REGISTERS AND LOGS

Delivery-Notice =

Document-Number + Document-Name + Document-Volume-Number + New/Update + Document-Type + Prepared-By + Submitted-By + Date-Submitted

Daily-Register =

Document-Number + Document-Name + Document-Volume-Number + New/Update + Document-Type + Prepared-By + Submitted-By + Date-Submitted

On-Site-Index =

Document-Number + Document-Name + Document-Volume-Number + Document-Type + Obsoletion-Date + Date-Filed + Filed-By + Type-of-Access + Term-of-Loan

Off-Site-Index =

Document-Number + Document-Name + Volume-Number + Document-Type + Original/Photocopy + Obsoletion-Date + Date-Obsoleted + Retention-Period + Date-Destroyed + Destroyed-By + Date-Filed + Filed-By + Off-Site-Location

Document-Processed-Log =

Document-Number + Document-Name + Volume-Number + New/Update + Original/Photocopy + Date-Processed

Document-Shipped-Off-Site-Register =

Document-Number + Document-Name + Volume-Number + New/Update + Original/Photocopy + Date-Shipped-Off-Site + Date-Retrieved-from-Off-Site

Charge-out-Card =

Document-Number + Document-Name + Volume-Number + User-Identification + Authorized-By + [Date-Charged-Out/Date-Returned/Date-Referenced]

History-Log =

Document-Number + Document-Name + Volume-Number + Date-Updated

User-Register =

User-Identification-Number + Name + Title + Location + Phone-Number

---

The output from Step 2 is the current system's logical data flow diagram, the normalized data structure diagram (data model), and the updated data dictionary. All of these combined together are termed the *current logical environment.* In this step, we eliminate all physical features in the Library System context, although we may not be able to get rid of physical entities from outside the system context. For example, the Delivery-Notice is created outside the system context and is retained. Let us examine some of the data flows in the present physical system diagrams (i.e., Figures 5.4 to 5.7).

In Figure 5.4, the inputs to bubble 1 are the Documentation and the Delivery-Notice. The Documentation consists of one or more volumes. Each volume is accompanied by a separate Delivery-Notice. Bubble 1 is Register Document. The function of Register Document is to record information about each Documentation-Volume. This information identifies the volume and provides necessary additional information about it, such as: Is it a new document or an update? Is it an archival document or is it a system document? Who prepared it? Who submitted it? When was it submitted? Much of this information is duplicated between the Documentation data flow and the Delivery-Notice data flow. Logically, we need to record only the net data. The input then becomes:

Documentation-Volume =

Document-Number + Document-Name + Document-Volume-Number + New/Update + Document-Type + Prepared-By + Submitted-By + Date-Submitted

When we design the new physical system in Step 4, this information will probably be captured from the Delivery-Notice.

Bubble 1 accesses two files. These are the Delivery-Notice storage file and the Daily Register. The Delivery-Notice storage file can be ignored as it is only a repository for the Delivery Notices. The Daily Register duplicates the information relating to Documentation-Volume.

Daily Register File =

Document-Number + Document-Name + Document-Volume-Number + New/Update + Document-Type + Prepared-By + Submitted-By + Date-Submitted

If, instead of several separate files, we assume we are working with one large file or data base, Daily Register File can be considered to be one user view or schema of this system file.

The output from bubble 1 is the Registered-Documentation-Volume, which has the same data content and structure as Documentation-Volume.

Registered-Documentation-Volume =

Document-Number + Document-Name + Document-Volume-Number + New/Update + Document-Type + Prepared-By + Submitted-By + Date-Submitted

To sum up, if we consider bubble 1 to be a black box, a record called Documentation-Volume is input which updates a file called Daily Register. The process also produces an output record called Registered-Documentation-Volume, which is an extract from the Daily Register file. This is illustrated in Figure 5.8.

In Figure 5.4, bubble 2 is Photocopy-Documentation, which produces two outputs, called Original-Documentation and Photocopy-Documentation.

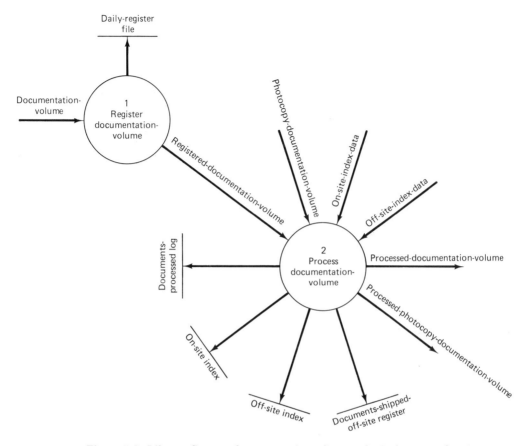

Figure 5.8 Library System documentation: Current logical system showing registration and processing only—diagram 0.

In our logical model, we are not concerned with the physical activity of photocopying. We are concerned only with the introduction of the Photocopy-Documentation-Volume record.

Photocopy-Documentation-Volume =

Document-Number + Photocopy-Document-Volume-Number + Date-Processed

We know from Figures 5.5 and 5.6 that processing includes updating the On-Site and Off-Site Indexes, creation of History Logs, preparation of Charge-out records, and completion of the Documents-Processed Log and the Documents-Shipped-Off-Site Register. Let us examine each of these in turn. In Figure 5.8, bubble 2 encompasses the logical processing of the original and the photocopy. It is exploded in Figure 5.9.

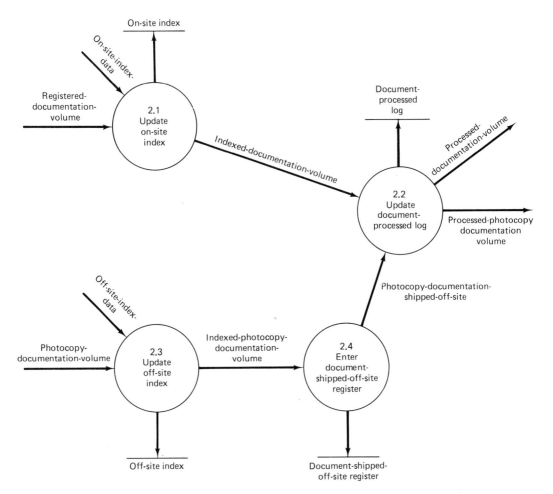

Figure 5.9 Library System documentation: Current logical system—diagram 2.

The On-Site and Off-Site Indexes are indexes of all Documentation-Volumes stored in the library. They contain information which is identical to the Documentation-Volume record and some additional data on the Obsoletion-Date, Date-Obsoleted, Retention-Period, Date-Destroyed, De-stroyed-By, Date-Filed, Filed-By, Off-Site-Location, Type-of-Access, and Term-of-Loan. Obviously, all these data are not available when the Documentation is processed, but become available later. All we have at this time is Date-Filed, Filed-By, the Off-Site-Location, Type-of-Access, and Term-of-Loan and hence the only data recorded. (We record the remaining data when they are processed.) The indices then become:

On-Site Index =

Document-Number + Document-Name + Document-Volume-Number + Document-Type + Date-Filed + Filed-By + Type-of-Access + Term-of-Loan

Off-Site Index =

Document-Number + Document-Name + Photocopy-Document-Volume-Number + Document-Type + Date-Filed + Filed-By + Off-Site-Location

The data in these indexes are input to bubble 2, Process Documentation-Volume, and also become user views or schemas in the system file. The History Log (Figure 5.4) tells us when each Update is added to the Documentation Volume. We can include the Date-Updated later when we analyze Updates to the Documentation. The Charge-out information (Figure 5.4) is identified only when the Charge-out Process is analyzed. We can ignore it now.

The only item of information we need now from the Documents-Shipped-Off-Site Register is Date-Shipped-Off-Site. The user view becomes

Documents-Shipped-Off-Site Register =

Document-Number + Photocopy-Document-Volume-Number + Date-Shipped-Off-Site

In Figure 5.9, the Indexed-Documentation-Volume and the Photocopy-Documentation-Volume-Shipped-Off-Site are input to bubble 2.2, called the Update Documentation-Processed Log. The file updated is the Document-Processed Log, which is a user view or schema in the system file.

Document-Processed Log =

Document-Number + Document-Volume-Number + Date-Processed + Original/Photocopy

Note: The Document-Volume-Number distinguishes between the original documentation and the photocopy (i.e., D1, D2 and P1, P2, etc.).

So far, we have analyzed only the data recorded in the files that will comprise the system file. We have not analyzed or recorded any of the logical data flows. Figure 5.8 is the present logical system level 0 diagram for the documentation registration and processing activities only. Figure 5.9 is the level 1 diagram for bubble 2, Process Documentation-Volume, in Figure 5.8. Table 5.2 is the normalized logical data dictionary, which has been copied from Table 4.6. Figure 5.10 is the data structure diagram (data model) showing the relationships between the logical records in Table 5.2. The reader may wish to complete the data flow diagrams and the data dictionary for the present logical system and develop a series of user views

TABLE 5.2   LOGICAL RECORD DATA DICTIONARY: NORMALIZED

Documentation =

Documentation-Identification-Number + Documentation-Name + Type-of-Access + Date-Written-Notice-to-Obsolete-Received + Obsoletion-Date + Date-Obsoleted + Retention-Period + Term-of-Loan

Documentation-Volume =

Documentation-Identification-Number + Documentation-Volume-Number + Date-Received + Date-Processed + Date-Filed + Prepared-By + Submitted-By + Date-Destroyed + Destroyed-By

Documentation-Charge-out =

Documentation-Identification-Number + Documentation-Volume-Number + Date-Documentation-Volume-Charged-Out + User-Identification-Number + Authorized-By + Date-Charged-In

Documentation-Reference =

Documentation-Identification-Number + Documentation-Volume-Number + Date-Documentation-Volume-Referenced + User-Identification-Number + Authorized-By

Documentation-Update =

Documentation-Identification-Number + Documentation-Update-Serial-Number + Prepared-By + Submitted-By + Date-Received + Date-Processed + Date-Filed + Filed-By

Photocopy-Documentation-Volume =

Documentation-Identification-Number + Photocopy-Documentation-Volume-Number + Date-Processed + Date-Shipped-Off-Site + Date-Filed + Filed-By + Off-Site-Location + Date-Destroyed + Destroyed-By

Photocopy-Update-Documentation =

Documentation-Identification-Number + Photocopy-Documentation-Update-Serial-Number + Date-Processed + Date-Shipped-Off-Site + Date-Filed + Filed-By

User

User-Identification-Number + Name + Title + Phone-Number

---

which can be normalized using canonical synthesis. He can then compare Figure 5.10 and Table 5.2 with his new normalized data model and the data dictionary.

At the end of Step 2, we have a series of data flow diagrams for the present logical system, an updated data dictionary containing the normalized system file, the data flows, and the related data structure diagram.

5.2.2.3 Deriving the new logical environment.   Now, in Step 3, we add the user's new requirements to the logical environment developed in Step 2.

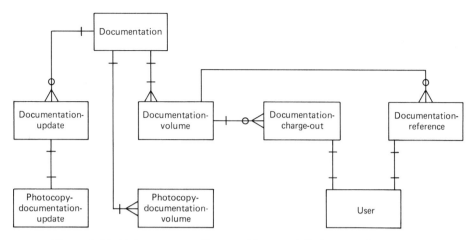

Figure 5.10 Data structure diagram (data model) showing the relationships between logical records in Table 5.2.

The new requirements could result in no change to the present logical environment (all that may be needed is a more efficient operation), the addition of new data and new processes, or the deletion of existing data and processes. If there is any change, the processes involved should be partitioned on the diagram and the analyst and user can concentrate their efforts on this partition. This partition now becomes the context diagram of the proposed system and everything else remains constant. In this step, we also describe the minispecifications for all the primitives in the data flow diagram covered by the new context. These are entered in the data dictionary.

In the Library System, the user's requirements were that the manual effort and the copying errors be reduced. There were no additional logical requirements. Hence the proposed logical system is the same as the present logical system.

Table 5.3 lists minispecifications for bubbles 2.1 and 2.2 in Figure 5.9. These are examples of the minispecifications that must be defined for each primitive in the proposed logical system.

5.2.2.4 Deriving the new physical environment. This step (Step 4) is the identification of different options to provide the required system covered by the new context. Each option may embrace different bubbles in the data flow diagram, depending on the degree and type of automation involved. In each case, the diagram is partitioned and the option described. These partitions distinguish between the people functions and the machine functions, hence the term *man/machine interface.* The outputs from this step are the physical options.

TABLE 5.3 LIBRARY SYSTEM:
EXAMPLES OF MINISPECIFICATIONS (FROM FIGURE 5.9)

Bubble 2.1 Update On-Site Index

Read On-Site-Index-Data record.
Match Document-Number and Document-Volume-Number with Document-Number and Document-Volume-Number in file.
   If not matched, reject On-Site-Index-Data record.
   If matched, update Documentation-Volume record.
      Add Date-Filed, Filed-By, Type-of-Access, Term-of-Loan.

Note: The Registered Documentation Volume data flow is unchanged during this process and has only a name change to Indexed-Documentation-Volume.

Bubble 2.2 Update Document-Processed Log

Read Indexed-Document-Volume record/Photocopy-Document-Shipped-Off-Site record.
Match Document-Number and Document-Volume-Number with Document-Number and Document-Volume-Number in file.
   If not matched, reject Indexed-Document-Volume record/Photocopy-Document-Shipped-Off-Site record.
   If matched, update Document-Volume-record/Photocopy-Document-Volume record.
      Add Date-Processed.

Note: The Indexed-Document-Volume record/Photocopy-Document-Shipped-Off-Site record is unchanged during this process and has only a name change to Processed-Document-Volume/Processed Photocopy-Document-Volume.

Four basic options were considered for the design of the new Library System:

1. Improve the existing manual procedures and files to reduce the duplication in effort.
2. Design an overnight batch system.
3. Design an interactive on-line system using COBOL as the programming language.
4. Design an interactive on-line system using FOCUS as the programming language.

The first option was discarded, as the improvement that could be achieved was limited and would not solve the problem. The second option was also discarded, as this would entail the preparation of manual records to answer queries during any one day period. As there is a heavy flow of material into and from the library, it was decided that the additional manual records would take up too much time. The third option and the fourth option were selected to be costed and scheduled.

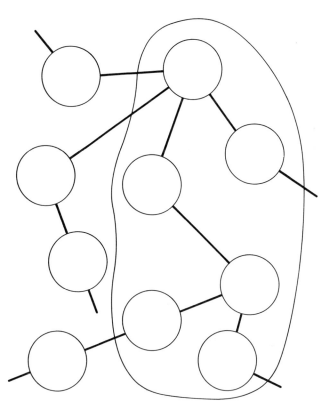

Figure 5.11 The man/machine interface.

Figure 5.11 is a data flow diagram partitioned to show how the "machine" activities are separated from the "man" activities. In the Library System, except for the keying of input in our options, the entire data flow diagram falls within the "machine" partition.

5.2.2.5 Cost and schedule design options.   Each design option is quantified in terms of cost/benefit and schedules. The outputs from this step (Step 5) are the costed options.

The cost of designing, building, and maintaining the Library System was as follows:

	COBOL	FOCUS
Systems analysts	6 person-months	2 person-months
User	1 person-month	6 person-months
Programmers	18 person-months	0 person-months
Data-base specialist	4 person-months	0 person-months
Maintenance annually	1 person-month	0.5 person-month
Conversion	6 person-months	6 person-months
Total first-year costs	35 person-months	14.5 person-months

Hardware (terminals, computer processing cycles, etc.) was not taken into account, as it was assumed that both options would require the same hardware and software support.

The estimated development time in the COBOL option was one year, while the FOCUS option was six months.

5.2.2.6 Selecting the design option. In this step (Step 6), the user selects the option best suited to his needs in terms of the cost/benefits and the development times. In the Library System, the user selected the FOCUS option based on cost, schedule, and the fact that the user could build and maintain the system himself with minimal support from a systems analyst.

5.2.2.7 Packaging option and supporting documents into the structured specification. The packaging (Step 7) could involve some or all of the following:

- Redrafting to call attention to key interfaces
- Preparing a structured specification guide to help the readers
- Preparing supplementary material to augment the specification
- Filling in details that have been deferred until now

Only the last item needs further comment. We add in information such as error messages, startup and shutdown procedures, control data and procedures, performance requirements, and conversion and implementation information. Last but not least, we ensure that statistical data that might be required from the files are included. As all this additional information could affect the data flow diagrams, the data structure diagram (data model), and the data dictionary, they should all be updated to reflect the additions. The output from this step is the packaged specification which is input to the system design phase of the total system life cycle.

The Library System documentation was cleaned up. Supporting details were added where necessary. The user verified that the system file structure could produce necessary statistical reports.

This completes structured analysis. We next convert the structured specification into a structured design.

5.3 STRUCTURED DESIGN

Before we proceed, let us see where structured design fits into the system life cycle. Figure 5.12 shows structured design as a process which has the structured specification from structured analysis and the hardware and software configuration input to it and produces an output called a packaged design, which, in turn, is input to the implementation process. In the implementa-

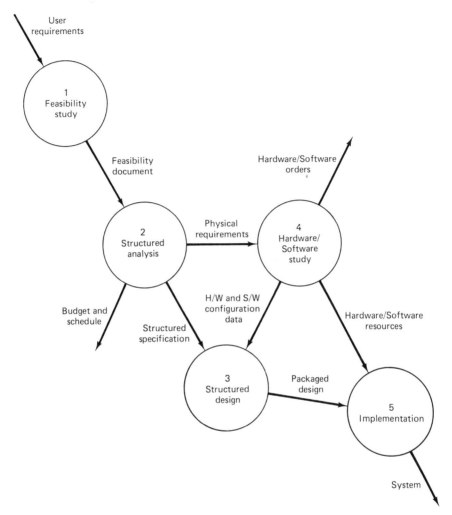

Figure 5.12 Structured analysis and design life cycle. Reprinted with the permission of Edward Yourdon.

tion process, the design is converted into code, the data structures into physical files, the pieces of the system and the whole system tested, and the system is put into production.

Figure 5.13 illustrates the processes in structured design. The first step is to design a structure chart based on the logical data flow diagram. The second step is to refine it. The third is to specify the logic (instructions) in the logical modules that make up the structure chart. The fourth is to package the modules and produce a set of physical modules and programs that can be coded during implementation.

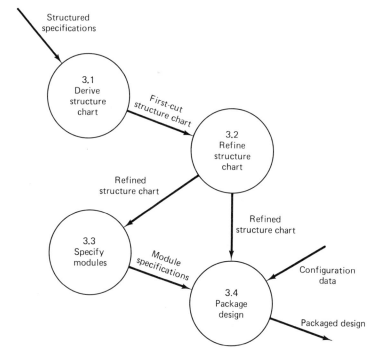

Figure 5.13 Structured design: Bubble 3 in Figure 5.12 exploded. Reprinted with the permission of Edward Yourdon.

5.3.1 Structure Chart

The structure chart (not to be confused with the structure diagram in Jackson system development) is the primary tool of structured design. What is a structure chart? A *structure chart* is a hierarchy of modules which call one another and pass data and control between them. Structure charts are a means of converting a system represented by a data flow diagram into a series of instructions that can be executed on a computer. Figure 5.14 illustrates the program described in Section 3.5 as a data flow diagram and as a structure chart. This structure chart identifies only the high-level modules in the process. Figures 5.15 to 5.17 expand (explode) these modules further.

The highest-level module in Figure 5.14 is "Accept Product-Order." This module controls the lower-level modules because it calls them and both obtains data from them and passes data to them. The link between the caller and the called is an arrow pointing at the called module. Data being passed are represented by a small circle attached to an arrow. When control is passed, it is also represented by a circle and arrow, but the circle is filled in. Control is a signal that a status has changed. For example, there are no more records to be read in a file; or one module can tell another that it has finished its activity and the second can now begin to execute.

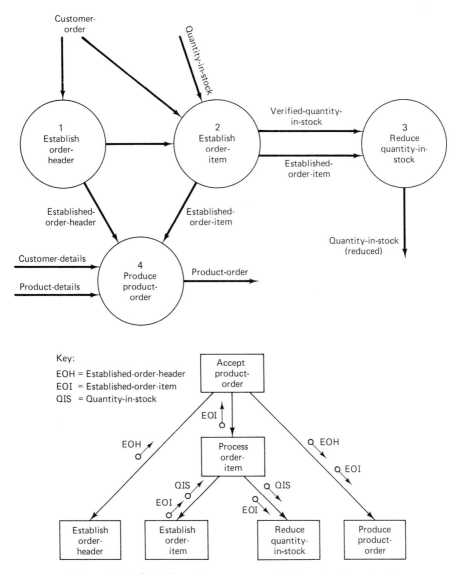

Figure 5.14 Data flow diagram converted to a structure chart.

In the data flow diagram, Customer-Order is input to bubble 1, Establish Order-Header, which processes it and produces the Established-Order-Header. In the structure chart, module Accept Product-Order tells module Establish Order-Header to get the EOH (Established-Order-Header). In Figure 5.15, Establish Order-Header calls module Get Customer-Number, which gets the data item CN (Customer-Number) and passes it to Establish Order-Header, which in turn passes it to Validate Customer-Number. Validate

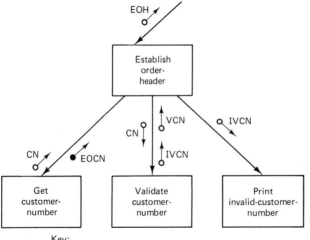

Key:

EOH   = Established-order-header
CN   = Customer-number
VCN   = Valid-customer-number
IVCN = Invalid-customer-number
EOCN = End-of-customer-number (no more orders)

Figure 5.15 Module "Establish Order Header" exploded.

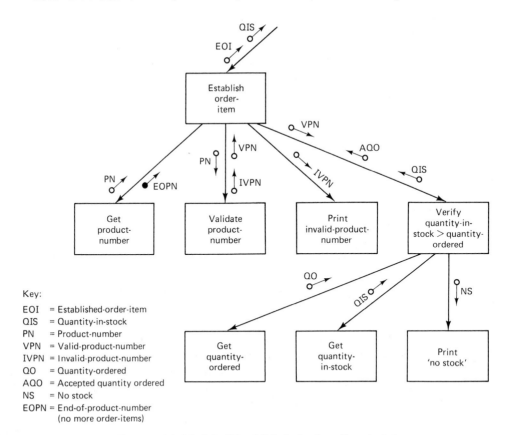

Key:

EOI   = Established-order-item
QIS   = Quantity-in-stock
PN   = Product-number
VPN   = Valid-product-number
IVPN = Invalid-product-number
QO   = Quantity-ordered
AQO   = Accepted quantity ordered
NS   = No stock
EOPN = End-of-product-number
        (no more order-items)

Figure 5.16 Module "Establish Order Item" exploded.

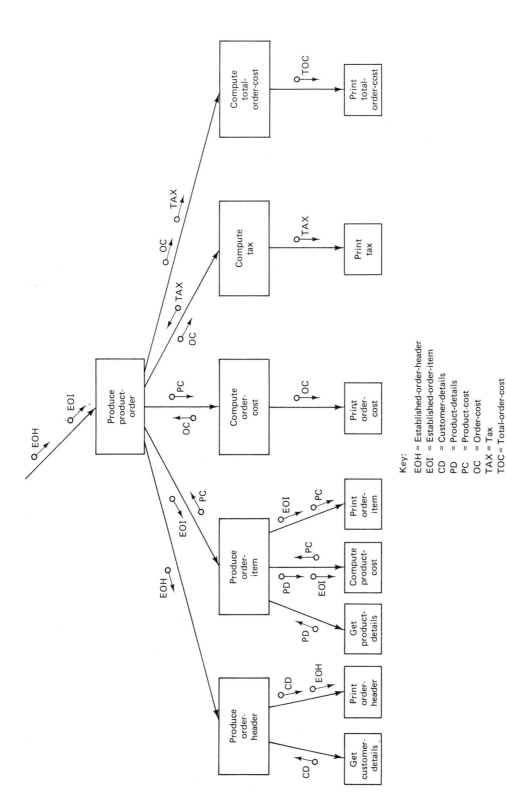

Figure 5.17 Module "Produce Product Order" exploded.

Key:

EOH = Established-order-header
EOI = Established-order-item
CD = Customer-details
PD = Product-details
PC = Product-cost
OC = Order-cost
TAX = Tax
TOC = Total-order-cost

Customer-Number validates Customer-Number and passes back either a valid or an invalid Customer-Number. If the number is invalid, Establish Order-Header passes the invalid number IVCN to Print Invalid-Customer-Number, which prints it. If the number is valid, it passes the Order-Header record called EOH (Established-Order-Header) to module Accept Product-Order. This example illustrates the relationship between a data flow diagram and a structure chart. The reader should compare the remaining data flows in Figure 5.14 with the movement of data in the structure charts in Figures 5.16 and 5.17.

In life, the only real producers in a people hierarchy should be the lowest workers in the hierarchy. Anyone above the lowest level should be in some type of supervisory or management position. The same principle applies in a structure chart. Only the lowest-level modules should actually change data. All other levels should only pass data between the lower levels or to and from the upper levels.

Structure charts can become very cluttered. This is evident from the simple program illustrated in Figures 5.14 to 5.17. To reduce this problem, whenever possible, different levels should be drawn in different diagrams.

5.3.2 Coupling

Coupling is a measure of interdependence between modules. The less dependence between modules, the less the chain reaction that occurs when a change occurs in a module's logic. Modules can be coupled in several ways. Let us examine some of them.

5.3.2.1 Data coupling. *Data coupling* is the passing of data between modules. Data coupling is essential, for with no data passed there is no system. It is possible to pass data through a module without actioning the module. This type of data is called *tramp data.* When tramp data occur, the module and the structure chart should be examined to see if the data can be eliminated from the affected module.

5.3.2.2 Stamp coupling. *Stamp coupling* occurs when entire records, rather than data items, are passed between modules. Because a change in a record structure can affect every module that accesses that record, it is preferable to pass data items only between modules, so that if a change in a record structure occurs that affects other data elements in a record, this module will not be affected.

5.3.2.3 Control coupling. *Control coupling* occurs when one module tells another module what to do. In Figure 5.15, EOCN (End-of-Customer-Number) is passed from "Get Customer-Number" to "Establish Order-Header." This tells "Establish Order-Header" that all the Customer-Numbers have been read. In other words, "repeat . . . until . . ." is complete. The passing of controls cannot be eliminated completely. The criterion used to assess whether the control should be passed or not is to attempt to carry out the control action required in the module passing the control. For example, one module encounters an error condition and tells the module below or above it to raise an error flag. This flag could be raised by the module encountering the error.

5.3.2.4 Common coupling.   *Common coupling* occurs when modules are coupled through global data areas such as the entire data structure, the data division in a COBOL program, and so on. It is a far worse situation than the one we encountered in stamp coupling.

5.3.2.5 Content coupling.   *Content coupling* occurs when an instruction in one module affects an instruction in another module (i.e., an "if" condition is reached that leads you out of one module to a "then" or an "else" statement in a completely different module). Can you imagine trying to debug or change a system with content coupling? This type of coupling is also referred to as *pathological coupling*.

5.3.3 Cohesion

Webster's New Collegiate Dictionary defines *cohesion* as "the act or process of sticking together tightly." In a module, this is a measure of its elements combining to execute the module's function or functions. There are seven different levels of cohesion, varying from very strong to very weak.

5.3.3.1 Functional cohesion.   A *functionally cohesive module* is one in which all the statements are directed at completing one function: for example, Read Customer record, Print Total, or Compute Quantity-in-Stock.

5.3.3.2 Sequential cohesion.   In *sequential cohesion*, the output from one task serves as input to the next: for example,

Compute Order-Cost
Compute Sales-Tax
Compute Total-Cost

Sequential cohesion is not as ideal as functional cohesion because it includes more than one function.

5.3.3.3 Communicational cohesion.   In *communicational cohesion*, different tasks perform different functions on the same input or output parameters. For example, Customer-Number is input and the functions performed are

Determine Customer-Name

Determine Customer-Salary

Modules displaying communicational cohesion should probably be split up.

5.3.3.4 Procedural cohesion. *Procedural cohesion* is similar to control coupling within a module. One statement follows another because the first is completed, but no data are passed. An example is

Print Order-Header

Print Order-Item

5.3.3.5 Temporal cohesion. *Temporal cohesion* is the inclusion of actions in a module because they occur at the same time but have no other connection. For example,

Rewind Tape Drive A

Rewind Tape Drive B

5.3.3.6 Logical cohesion. *Logical cohesion* is the opposite of what the name implies. It refers to modules in which statements appear to be logically grouped but in fact are not. For example,

If employee = manager
    Increase salary by 10%.
If employee = secretary
    Vacational entitlement = 3 weeks.
If employee = janitor
    Working hours from 8 A.M. to 5 P.M.

This example is not as ridiculous as it appears to be because it links employees and employees' benefits. The problem is that the benefits are completely unrelated. A common programming example is where a module lists a series of flags and the action to be taken on each flag, but none of the flags are related.

5.3.3.7 Coincidental cohesion. *Coincidental cohesion* is exactly that. This type of cohesion was very common in the early days of program modularization when large chunks of program code were "modularized." The reason the statements were grouped was because someone arbitrarily did so to break the program into smaller pieces.

To sum up, functional and sequential cohesion are the only two types of cohesion that should be accepted in a module. Any other type, when recognized, should be analyzed to see if the module can be changed to be functional or sequential. This could entail restructuring of modules and structure charts.

5.3.4 Refining the Structure Chart

Refining the structure chart is the second step in the structured design process. In it, we examine the structure chart and the modules to obtain the minimum of coupling and the maximum of cohesion. It also involves some "housekeeping." The following are common types of refinement.

5.3.4.1 Factoring. *Factoring* is the separation of management-type actions, such as decision making or calling, from work-type actions such as calculating and validating. Figure 5.18 illustrates the use of factoring. In the

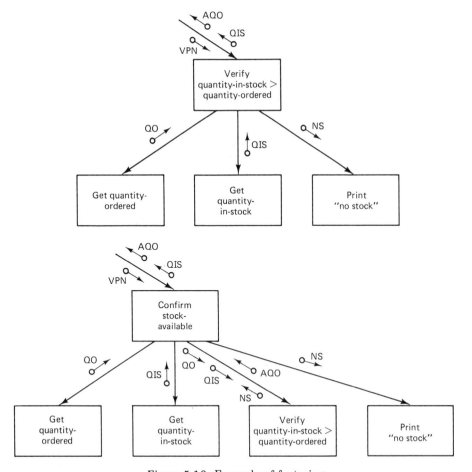

Figure 5.18 Example of factoring.

upper structure chart, the management module does work (i.e., it verifies that the Quantity-in-Stock is greater than the Quantity-Ordered). In the lower structure chart, this function is "factored" out and is carried out by a worker module.

5.3.4.2 Decision splitting.   A decision has two parts:

1. Recognition of what action to take
2. Execution of that action

A decision is split when the recognition and the execution affect different entities. For example,

> If Customer-Number is invalid
>   Then reject Order-Item.

(Customer-Number is a data element in the Customer-Order record but is not part of Order-Item.)

5.3.4.3 Fan-out (span of control).   In management, it is generally accepted that no manager should supervise more than seven people. So also, no manager module should have more than seven other modules under its control. High fan-out can be reduced by introducing middle-management modules between the manager and the workers.

5.3.4.4 Overgeneral modules.   *Overgeneral modules* are modules designed to cope with complex situations where simple situations will do, or where every possible alternative is covered off when 90% of them rarely occur, if they occur at all.

5.3.4.5 Error reporting.   Some designers have a tendency to report all errors through one module even though they are not related. Errors should be reported where and when they occur. On the other hand, it is a good idea to keep error messages together and to call this "print" module whenever an error message is to be printed. This controls the messages and ensures consistency.

5.3.4.6 Fan-in.   *Fan-in* occurs when common modules, such as the error message module just referred to, are called. Fan-in, when used effectively, avoids reinventing the wheel.

5.3.4.7 System shape.   The best system shape for a structure chart is the "mosque" or "onion" shape. This implies a single module at the top which widens through the management hierarchy and reaches its widest point at the worker level, when it turns inward toward the common modules. Inside this structure, the modules should be grouped like the McDonald's (hamburgers) "M." The left arm contains the input modules, called *afferent modules*. The dip in the middle is the *transform*, where processing occurs. The right arm contains the output modules, called *efferent modules*. In real life, a perfect mosque or onion shape rarely occurs.

5.3.4.8 Information-hiding modules.   When dealing with complex data structures such as data-base management systems, access modules can be designed which accept calls for data from the application system and obtain these data from the data-base management system. The application system processes the data and returns them to the access module, which updates the data base. The use of these access modules protects the application system modules from changes made in the data base.

5.3.5 Transform Analysis

Up to this point, we have looked at structure charts from all angles but have not discussed how to convert a data flow diagram into a structure chart. This conversion is done using two tools, called transform analysis and transaction analysis. *Transform analysis* deals with the conversion of data flow diagrams for sequential processes. *Transaction analysis* deals with the conversion of transactions. Often, data flow diagrams portray both sequential- and transaction-type processes. When this occurs, we combine both types of analysis.

Figure 5.19 is a data flow diagram for a system for paying accident claims. The steps followed are:

1. Register claim.
2. Investigate claim.
3. Accept claim.
4. Update customer record.
5. Pay claim.

This data flow diagram can be divided into three parts:

1. Afferent or input
2. Central transform
3. Efferent or output

In this example, it is not difficult to identify the central transform; it is Accept Claim. In more complex data flow diagrams, the central transform could embrace several bubbles. Mark the diagram to isolate the central

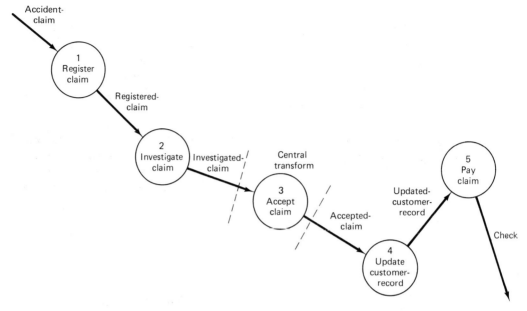

Figure 5.19 A data flow diagram illustrating a "Central Transform."

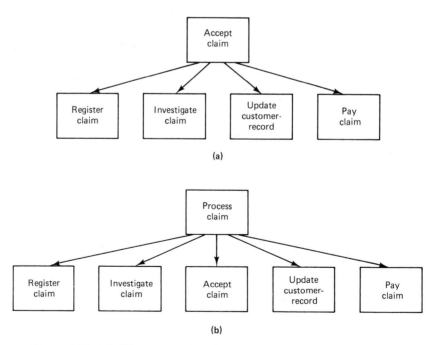

Figure 5.20 (a) "Promote a Boss" and (b) "Hire a New Boss" approaches to drawing structure charts.

transform. From here on, we have two choices: We can promote a "boss" module or we can hire a new boss module. Figure 5.20 illustrates both approaches. The "hire a new boss" approach ensures that the manager module does not perform any work except to direct data. But from a practical viewpoint, it might be preferable on occasion to use the "promote the boss approach."

Let us look at what we have done. Initially, we identified the central transform. Next, we lifted up the data flow diagram by the central transform and let the afferent and efferent bubbles hang down from it. If we decide to use the "hire a new boss" approach, we let the central transform hang down as well. Each bubble becomes a module. From this point on, we can explode each module to its lowest level of detail.

5.3.6 Transaction Analysis

Figure 5.21 is a data flow diagram for an automated bank teller system. A customer inserts his individualized card into the machine.

1. The machine validates the card.

The customer keys in a personal identification which prevents misuse of a stolen card.

2. The machine validates the personal number.

The customer now has a menu of transactions he can choose from. He makes his choice and begins:

3. He identifies the transaction, which could be:
   4. Deposit money.
   5. Withdraw money.
   6. Pay bills.
   7. Transfer between accounts.
8. The machine tells him that the transaction is complete and gives him a choice of finishing or starting another transaction.
9. The machine returns the customer's card.

A *transaction center* in a data flow diagram is a set of processes where each process can occur independent of every other process in the set. In our example, the transaction center extends from bubble 3 to bubble 8. Figure 5.22 illustrates how this transaction center is converted to a structure chart. The transform center is given a boss module and each transaction hangs down from this boss. The black diamond in the boss identifies the transaction center.

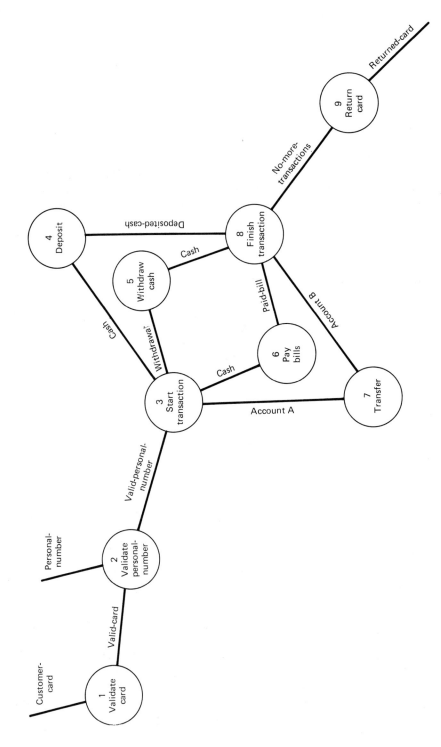

Figure 5.21 Data flow diagram illustrating "Transactions."

114

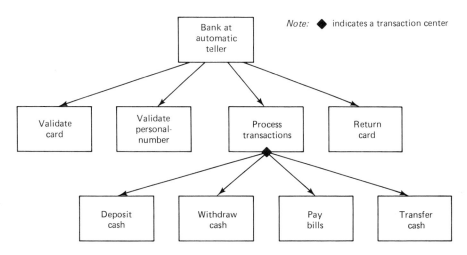

Figure 5.22 Structure chart illustrating a "Transaction Center."

5.3.7 Module Specification

The primitive bubbles in the data flow diagram were described using the three basic constructs—sequence, selection, and iteration—using structured English. We define the modules in the same fashion. Some analysts may choose to use pseudocode instead of structured English. (Pseudocode is a more specific form of structured English which can easily be converted to a programming language such as COBOL. Fourth-generation languages such as FOCUS do not need to be specified in pseudocode.)

5.3.8 Packaging Physical Modules

A *physical module* is an entity which can be called by or become part of a program. For example, in COBOL a physical module could be a paragraph in the procedure division. The question could be asked: "Why package?" We package because packaging gives us manageable sets of process instructions which perform related functions. If we did not package, we could make every logical module a separate physical entity or, at the other extreme, we could make the entire structure chart into one entity. Neither of these is very practical—so we package. But in packaging, we do not lose control over the logical modules. Figure 5.23 illustrates the same structure chart with good and poor packaging. Good packaging occurs when the packages encompass modules in parent-child relationships.

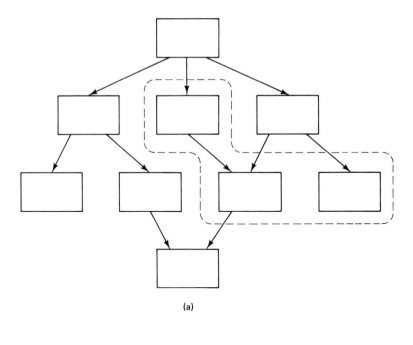

(a)

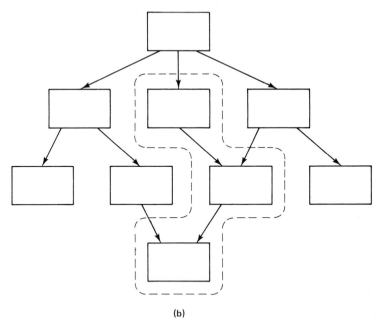

(b)

Figure 5.23 (a) Poor and (b) good module packaging.

5.3.9 The Library System

The last time we looked at the Library System was in structured analysis. Figures 5.8 and 5.9 illustrate the logical processes for registration and processing. Using the "hire a boss approach," we produce the structure chart shown in Figure 5.24. Let us examine it.

The manager module Accept Documentation calls Register Documentation, which executes and passes a record called Registered-Documentation-

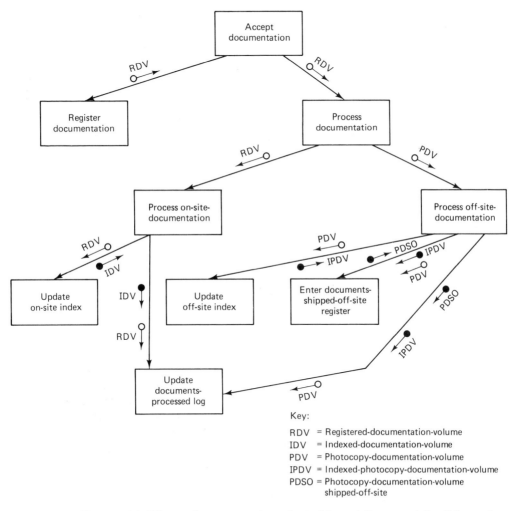

Key:

RDV = Registered-documentation-volume
IDV = Indexed-documentation-volume
PDV = Photocopy-documentation-volume
IPDV = Indexed-photocopy-documentation-volume
PDSO = Photocopy-documentation-volume
          shipped-off-site

Figure 5.24 Library System structure chart. "Accept Documentation" for register and process documentation from Figures 5.8 and 5.9.

Volume to Accept Documentation, which passes it to module Process Documentation. Process Documentation executes and produces a record called Photocopy-Documentation-Volume, which it passes to module Process Off-Site-Documentation. Module Process Documentation also passes Registered-Documentation-Volume to module Process On-Site-Documentation, which passes it to module Update On-Site Index. Update On-Site Index executes and passes a control called Indexed-Documentation-Volume to Process On-Site-Documentation, which passes it along with Registered-Documentation-Volume to module Update Documents Processed Log, which executes.

Beginning with Process Off-Site Documentation, a similar series of actions takes place. To complete the structure chart, each module should be exploded to its lowest levels of detail just as we did in Figures 5.14 to 5.17. This has been done for modules Register Documentation, Update On-Site Index, and Update Documents-Processing Log in Figure 5.25 to 5.27.

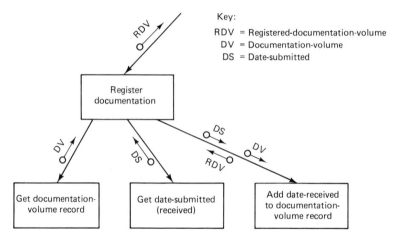

Figure 5.25 Module "Register Documentation" exploded.

What have we achieved through this process? We have established a Documentation-Volume record and have added Registration, On-Site Index, and Processing data to it. We have also established a Photocopy-Documentation-Volume record and have added Registration, Off-Site-Index, Documents-Shipped-Off-Site, and Processing data to it.

The structure chart passes whole records instead of data items and so is guilty of stamp coupling. It passes controls between modules and so is guilty of control coupling. Let us return now to our data structure diagram, Figure 5.10. Here we find a record called Documentation which contains data found in our expanded Documentation-Volume and Photocopy-Documentation-Volume records. For the reader's benefit, these three records are reproduced below from Table 5.2.

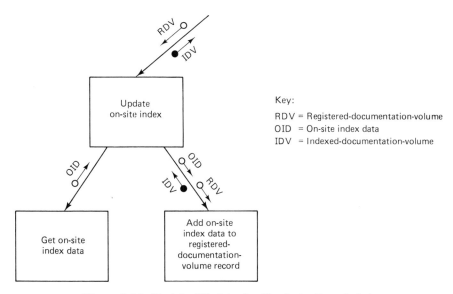

Figure 5.26 Module "Update On-Site Index" exploded.

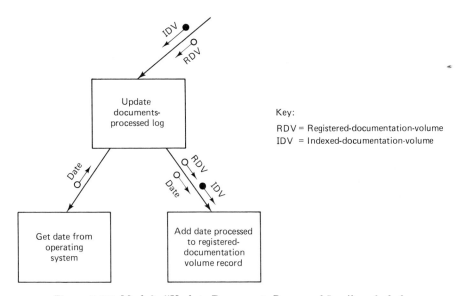

Figure 5.27 Module "Update Documents Processed Log" exploded.

Documentation =

<u>Documentation-Identification-Number</u> + Documentation-Name + Type-of-Access +   Date-Written-Notice-to-Obsolete-Received + Obsoletion-Date + Date-Obsoleted + Retention-Period + Term-of-Loan

Documentation-Volume =

<u>Documentation-Identification-Number</u> + <u>Documentation-Volume-Number</u> + Date-Received + Date-Processed + Date-Filed + Prepared-By + Submitted-By + Date-Destroyed + Destroyed-By

Photocopy-Documentation-Volume =

<u>Documentation-Identification-Number</u> + <u>Photocopy-Documentation-Volume-Number</u> + Date-Processed + Date-Shipped-Off-Site + Date-Filed + Filed-By + Off-Site-Location + Date-Destroyed + Destroyed-By

Now that we know this and know that we have infringed on some of the coupling guidelines, it is time to take a second look at the structure chart. Figure 5.28 is another approach to solving this problem based on the records in the data structure diagram.

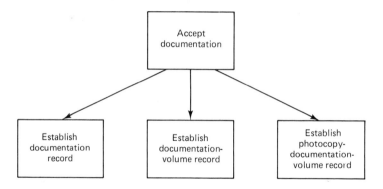

Figure 5.28 Structure chart "Accept Documentation" reworked to eliminate flow of data and control.

We have the same Accept Documentation manager module. We also have three new modules, called

Establish Documentation Record
Establish Documentation-Volume Record
Establish Photocopy-Documentation Record

These three modules are completely independent, functionally cohesive, and pass no data or controls. They also provide all the data that we need. This is an example of how the organization and content of a structure chart can be changed when the structure chart is refined.

5.3.10 Implementation

Implementation is not part of the structured design process. We mention it here because implementation following structured design is heavily influenced by the structured design. With a structured design, the implementer has three routes he can follow to develop and test the system: He can start from the top and build a framework of manager modules where he can test their interfaces and add on modules at lower and lower levels until complete subsystems and the entire system are tested. He can start from the bottom and keep adding higher-level modules. Or, he can use a sandwich approach and start at both ends. He can achieve all this testing using test software to simulate the modules not yet coded. Two terms are used to describe manager- and worker-simulated modules. The managers are called *drivers* and the workers are called *stubs*.

5.4 ADVANTAGES AND DISADVANTAGES OF STRUCTURED ANALYSIS AND DESIGN

Advantages

1. The most important feature of structured analysis and design is the step-by-step evolution of the analysis and the design. We begin with the present physical system, convert it into the present logical system, and in the process develop a normalized data structure eliminating all duplicate and unnecessary data. We convert this logical system to the proposed logical system by adding in the new system requirements. This system provides us with a framework to specify a new physical system. This physical system becomes the basis for the new system design, which in turn drives the testing and implementation.

2. Throughout the process, we deal with manageable pieces of information which can be effectively controlled.

3. The hierarchical design approach provides a well-organized and manageable system.

4. The refinement of the structure charts provides modules which are independent and functional.

Disadvantages

1. The biggest disadvantage is the large amount of data that must be recorded and controlled. We could have the same data defined in many different ways because of an action taken on it or a change in data values. (Every data flow, including those with identical data, must be defined at least through a cross-reference.) This duplication cannot be

avoided because it is a fundamental principle of the structured analysis and design process. The same type of problem occurs in the structure charts, which can become very messy and hard to maintain because of the large amounts of data and controls being passed from module to module.

2. The data structure diagram (data model) is a by-product of the process and hence can change if the process changes. This could create problems when working with complex systems and very large files or data bases.

3. When the structured analysis process evolves from the present physical to the present logical, all time-oriented features of the system are lost, such as daily, weekly, or on-demand requirements. These are touched on again in the proposed physical design but are really dealt with only when the logical modules are packaged. In the meantime, we could have separated processes which belong together in time. This makes packaging a task that requires considerable skill.

4. The principle of data conservation requires lower-level data flows to be children of higher-level data flows (i.e., the higher-level data flows are composed of the lower-level data flows). Even using an effective data dictionary software package, this is a difficult and time-consuming task in which errors can easily occur.

REFERENCES

1. Tom DeMarco, *Structured Analysis and System Specification*, Prentice-Hall, Inc., Englewood Cliffs, NJ, 1979. Copyright © 1978, 1979 YOURDON, INC. See pp. 16, 47, and 215–226.

2. Edward Yourdon and Larry L. Constantine, *Structured Design*, Prentice-Hall, Inc., Englewood Cliffs, NJ, 1979.

3. Glenford J. Myers, *Composite Structured Design*, Van Nostrand Reinhold Company, Inc., New York, 1978.

Structured Requirements Definition

6.1 WHAT IS STRUCTURED REQUIREMENTS DEFINITION?

Structured systems development is defined by Ken Orr in the book *Structured Systems Development* [1] as "output oriented design." In other words, a system is designed to provide the outputs the user needs to do his job. In *Structured Requirements Definition* [2], Orr expands on this principle. He states that "it is not always possible to elicit the required outputs from the user." So we must have "a requirements definition process that works from a definition of the problem to the definition of the outputs. But even this is not enough. It is also necessary to develop a planning and definition phase that moves from an initial problem statement (symptoms) to correct definition of the problems and scope (systems identification)." In essence, the structured requirements definition approach to system design provides "mandatory outputs defined by a rigorous requirements definition process." To appreciate this objective, we must define exactly what we mean by the term "output."

Systems are designed and built to satisfy management objectives. These objectives are met by certain functions being performed. These functions require data in a format where they can be used. These formatted data are what we term the *output*. Output can be in the form of a report, a check, an invoice, an inquiry screen, and even a file or data base. Files and data bases are often not thought of as outputs. Their importance as outputs is emphasized in systems which serve as controls or which support decision making where it is not practical to define all the possible reports that might be required. The tools used in structured requirements definition are the Warnier-Orr diagram and the entity diagram.

6.2 WARNIER-ORR DIAGRAMS

The *Warnier-Orr diagram* is an analysis and design tool which uses braces to display hierarchical systems. The term "system" here embraces all systems. For example, it can display an organization, a computer system, a computer program, a data structure, or a set of manual procedures. It resembles a family tree, but instead of being vertical, it is horizontal. It is based on the principle that a "single" parent can have "many" children and a child can have only "one" parent.

6.2.1 Data Structure Diagram

We stated that structured requirements definition is an output-driven analysis and design technique. So, for our first example, let us look at an output. Figure 6.1 is a Customer Order form which contains data produced by a computer process. The data in the form identify the Order; the Customer; the details of the products ordered, called the Order Items; and the Costs. Figure 6.2 portrays the same data in the form of a Warnier-Orr diagram. Here we find a brace enclosing the data items that make up the Order Header and a second brace enclosing the data items that make up an Order Item. We also note that there must be at least and at most N Order Items. This is indicated by the $(1,N)$ beneath the Order Item. A third brace encloses the tax and cost data. A large brace encompasses the first three, and this represents the Customer Order.

Figure 6.2 tells us that a Customer Order has three records, called the Order Header, the Order Item, and the Order End, and the entire diagram represents the data structure for the Customer Order. So, Customer Order is the single parent and Order Header, Order Item, and Order End are the children. We also note that Order Header and Order End each occur once for each Customer Order, and Order Item occurs at least once but can occur up to N times. In turn, Order Header, Order Item, and Order End each have children which are their data items. A data structure is one application of a Warnier-Orr diagram.

6.2.2 System and Process Diagrams

Let us look at another application. The Customer Order is produced as an output from a process called Process Customer Order. This process is essentially the same process as that encountered in Section 3.5 except that we

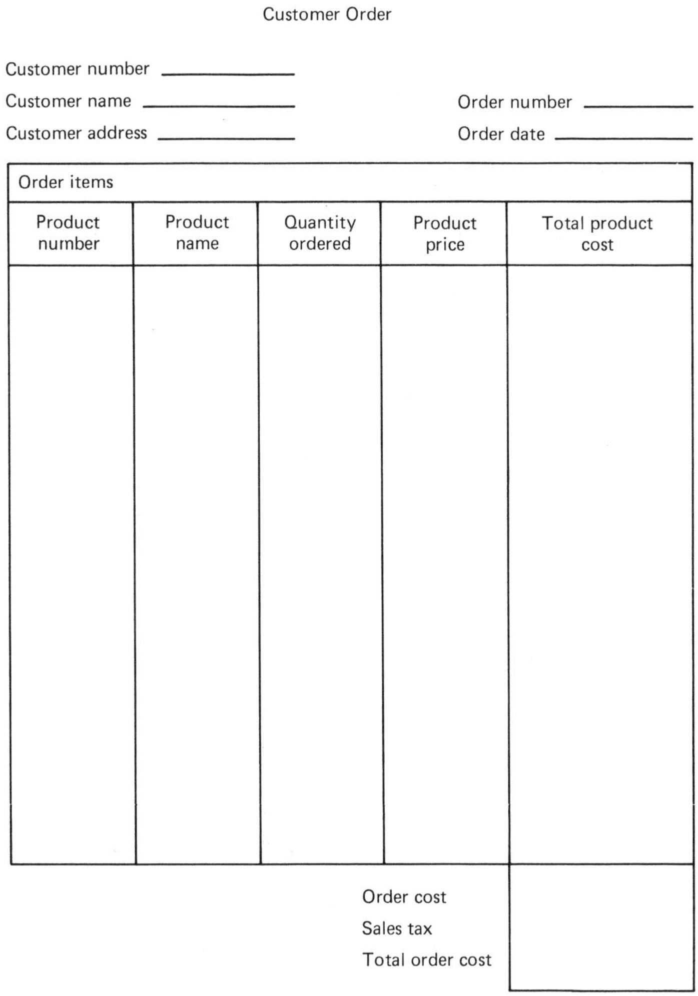

Customer Order

Customer number _____

Customer name _____   Order number _____

Customer address _____   Order date _____

Order items				
Product number	Product name	Quantity ordered	Product price	Total product cost
			Order cost	
			Sales tax	
			Total order cost	

Figure 6.1 Example of an output "Customer Order."

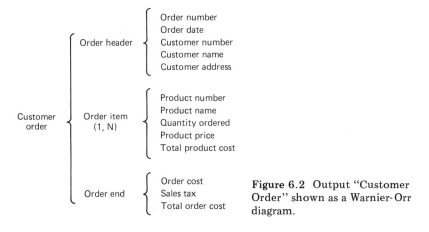

Figure 6.2 Output "Customer Order" shown as a Warnier-Orr diagram.

have added a Date to the Order Header record. Figure 6.3 lists its steps using a Warnier-Orr diagram. The reader will note that the process has essentially the same structure as the Customer Order form's data structure, except that instead of Order End we have Print Order. Further, if we divided the process into two parts, the first part, Begin Order and Order Body, reflects the Customer Order's data structure in terms of the file update, while the second part, Print Order, reflects the same data structure for the printing of the form.

The reader should note that in the Warnier-Orr data structure diagram, the lowest data levels are on the right and the highest on the left. In the

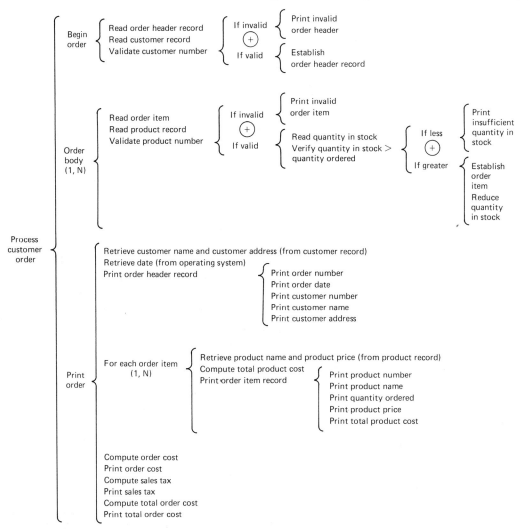

Figure 6.3 Example of a process shown as a Warnier-Orr diagram.

Warnier-Orr process diagram, the instructions start at the left and move to the right.

The reader might note the resemblance between the Warnier-Orr process description and the DAD (data-base action diagram) in Figure 4.15, which lists the first half of the same process. They both follow the same hierarchical principle; only the notation is different.

6.2.3 Assembly Line Diagram

The *assembly line diagram* combines data and process. Figure 6.4 illustrates how it works. The assembly line diagram is a very powerful application of the Warnier-Orr diagram. Later, we will see how the assembly line diagram is used to describe subsystems and complete systems. These diagrams not only define the inputs, outputs, and the processes, but also define the time frames governing the subsystems.

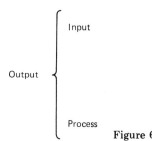

Figure 6.4 Assembly line diagram.

6.2.4 Warnier-Orr Diagram Notation

Figure 6.5 provides examples of the more common applications of the notation.

Sequence is shown by a brace embracing the sequential steps.

Repetition implies that a step can occur zero or many times. "Do" Step 2 "until" a condition is satisfied is shown as (1,s). This means that the step must occur at least once before the condition is satisfied. "Do" Step 2 "while" a condition is being satisfied is shown as (0,s). This means that the step can occur zero or many times, depending on the condition being met. A variation of this situation is the optional step shown by (0,1).

A *selection* or branching caused by an "if" condition is shown by a + sign enclosed in a circle. A negative condition is indicated by a bar over the condition.

Concurrency implies that steps occur together or in sequence. But either step can occur first. This is indicated by a + sign.

Recursion implies an update where an earlier version has something added and produces the new version.

Arithmetic operators are shown with the operator enclosed in a box.

Record content is shown with a brace and the keys are underlined.

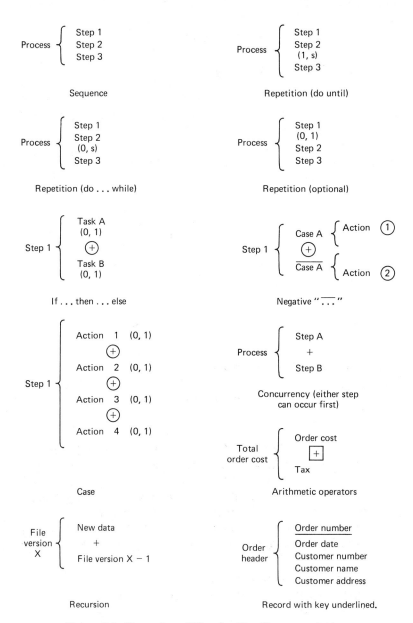

Figure 6.5 Examples of Warnier-Orr diagram notation.

6.2.5 Warnier-Orr Diagrams versus Data Flow Diagrams

In Chapter 5 we learned that a data flow diagram is a tool that displays a system as a network and that any bubble in the network can have many inputs and many outputs. This can apply even at the primitive bubble level. A Warnier-Orr diagram is a hierarchy and not a network. Hence any process in it can have only one output, although it can have many inputs. This makes the process "functional" (see Section 5.3.3.1). So, using Warnier-Orr diagrams in our system ensures the design of functional processes. We do not have this assurance using data flow diagrams. Figure 6.6 shows the inputs and outputs for a bubble in a data flow diagram converted to a series of Warnier-Orr diagrams and illustrates the production of single outputs.

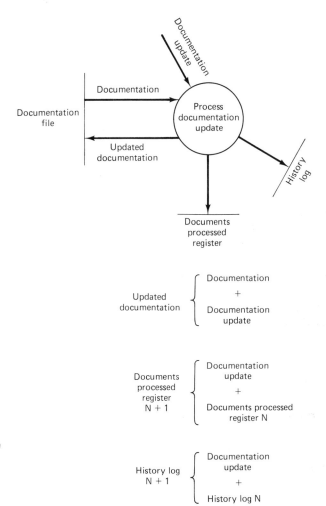

Figure 6.6 Inputs and outputs for a data flow diagram bubble converted to Warnier-Orr diagrams.

6.3 REQUIREMENTS DOCUMENT

The structured requirements definition process is based on the definition of the outputs. Before we examine this process, it is appropriate that we define the outputs or the end result we can expect from the process. These are:

- Definition of the principal outputs from the system. This includes the layouts, samples, data structure, process logic, volumes, frequencies, and response times.
- Dictionary of data definitions for logical files, logical records, data items, and data structures.
- Definition of the assumptions and constraints involved in the system.
- Definition of the risks and benefits of the various approaches.

The total process is divided into two phases:

1. Logical definition phase
2. Physical definition phase

6.4 LOGICAL DEFINITION PHASE

The *logical definition phase* has three steps:

1. Define the application context.
2. Define the application functions.
3. Define the application results in the form of principal outputs.

The context provides us with the system scope, the system's users, the principal flows of data between the users, and the actions taken by the users. Orr calls these actions *objectives*: for example, "Receive orders" from customers and "Send invoices" to customers. We will refer to these actions as "objectives" in this chapter.

6.4.1 Application Context Definition

The *application context definition* consists of four steps:

1. Define a user-level entity diagram for each user.
2. Define a combined user-level entity diagram.

3. Define the application-level entity diagram.
4. Define the objectives.

We have just encountered the term "entity" again. In structured requirements definition, "entity" means "user." An *entity* is any person or any organizational group within the organization or outside it who receives or passes data through the system.

6.4.1.1 User-level entity diagram.   The *user-level entity diagram* is drawn as follows:

1. Put the organization's name, the user's name, and the system's name at the top of the page.
2. Create a bubble in the middle of the page and write the user's name in the bubble.
3. Draw in bubbles around the edge of the page and write in the entities (other users) with which the user will interface in this system.
4. Draw arrows linking the user in the middle with the other entities, showing the interactions (transactions) between them.

Before we draw entity diagrams for the Library System, let us examine a simple Accounts Receivable System. This system links the Accounts Receivable Section, the Shipping Department, the Sales Department, and the Customer. Figures 6.7, 6.8, and 6.9 are entity diagrams for the Accounts Receivable Section, the Shipping Department, and the Sales Department.

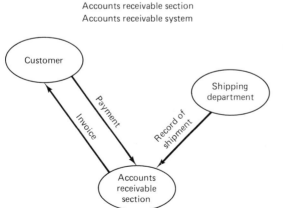

Figure 6.7 Entity diagram:
Accounts Receivable Section.

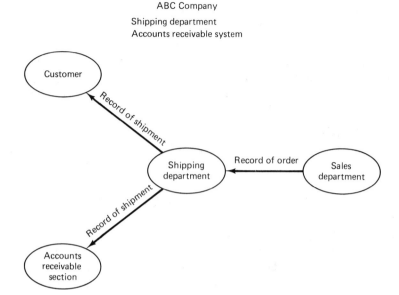

Figure 6.8 Entity diagram: Shipping Department.

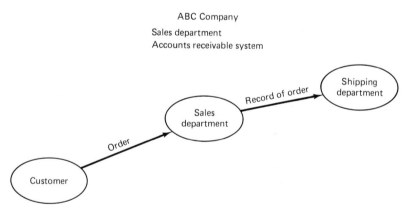

Figure 6.9 Entity diagram: Sales Department.

6.4.1.2 Combined user-level entity diagram.   The entity diagrams for each user are combined into a single diagram called a combined user-level entity diagram. Figure 6.10 illustrates how the diagrams are combined for the Accounts Receivable System.

6.4.1.3 Application-level entity diagram.   Certain entities only will be included in the application system to be developed. A boundary is drawn around these entities and this provides us with the application-level entity

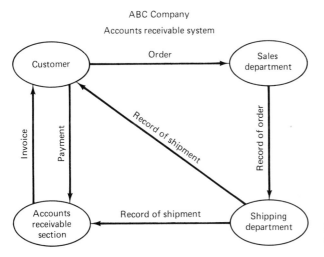

Figure 6.10 Combined user-level entity diagram.

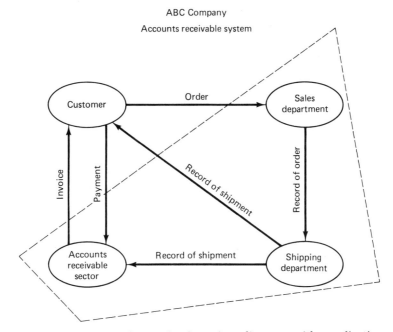

Figure 6.11 Combined user-level entity diagram with application boundary.

diagram. Figure 6.11 shows the application boundaries drawn and Figure 6.12 shows the entire application represented by a single bubble, here called the Company. (The reader will recall the context diagram in structured analysis, which fulfilled a similar function.) This single bubble provides the application context.

ABC Company

Accounts receivable system

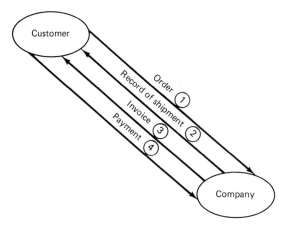

Figure 6.12 Application-level entity diagram.

6.4.1.4 System objectives. What functions should this system perform? These functions are termed *objectives* because they produce measurable results. We define these objectives by inspecting the application-level entity diagram. The objectives in the Accounts Receivable System are listed in Figure 6.13.

1. Receive orders (from customers)
2. Send shipments (to customers)
3. Send invoice (to customers)
4. Receive payments (from customers)

Figure 6.13 Accounts Receivable System application objectives.

Before we proceed any further, let us draw the various level entity diagrams and define the objectives for the Library System.

6.4.1.5 The Library System. In the Library System, we have three user entities. These are the Library Users, the Systems Library On-Site, and the Systems Library Off-Site. As there is no direct interaction between the Library Users and the Systems Library Off-Site, drawing the entity diagram for the Systems Library On-Site gives us the combined user-level entity diagram. This diagram is shown in Figure 6.14. In Figure 6.15 we draw the application boundary, and produce the application-level entity diagram in Figure 6.16. This diagram shows the same interactions between the Library Users and the Systems Library as existed between the Library Users and the Systems Library On-Site. The reason for this duplication is that from the Library User's viewpoint, the interactions between the Library On-Site and

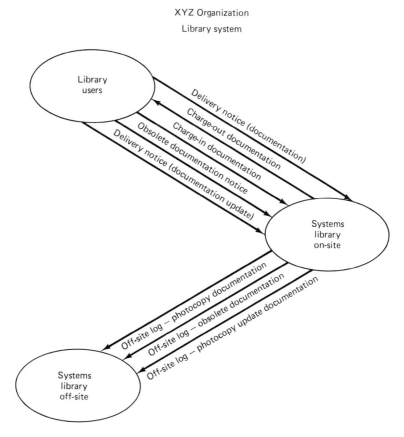

Figure 6.14 Combined user-level entity diagram.

the Library Off-Site are transparent. In other words, the Library User inter-
acts only with the Library On-Site and is not concerned with the movement
of material and information between the on-site and off-site locations.

The interactions between the Library Users and the Systems Library
are:

1. Delivery Notice submitted with the Documentation by the user to the
   library
2. Charge-out or loan of Documentation by the user
3. Charge-in or return of Documentation by the user
4. Delivery of the Obsolete Documentation Notice by the user
5. Delivery Notice submitted with Documentation Update by the user

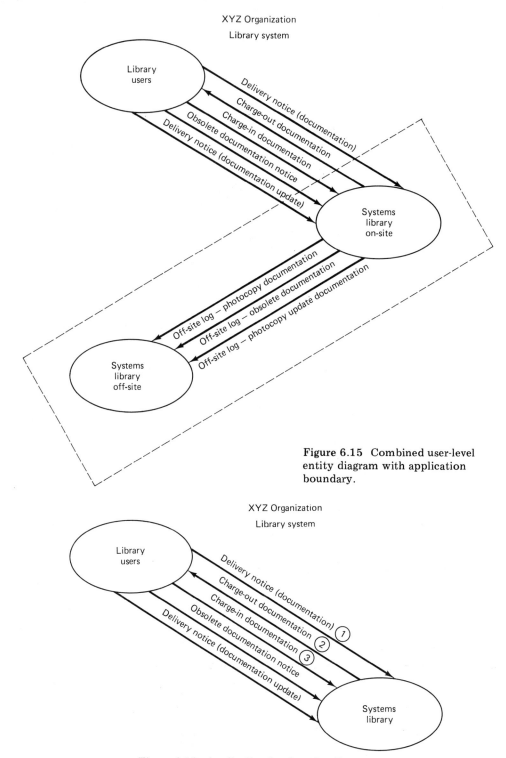

XYZ Organization

Library system

Library users

Delivery notice (documentation)

Charge-out documentation

Charge-in documentation

Obsolete documentation notice

Delivery notice (documentation update)

Systems library on-site

Off-site log — photocopy documentation

Off-site log — obsolete documentation

Off-site log — photocopy update documentation

Systems library off-site

Figure 6.15 Combined user-level entity diagram with application boundary.

XYZ Organization

Library system

Library users

Delivery notice (documentation)

Charge-out documentation ①

Charge-in documentation ②

Obsolete documentation notice ③

Delivery notice (documentation update)

Systems library

Figure 6.16 Application-level entity diagram.

In every case, the action has been taken by the user and the library has played a passive role. The corresponding objectives are listed in Figure 6.17.

1. Receive documentation (from users)
2. Charge-out documentation (to users)
3. Charge-in documentation (from users)
4. Obsolete documentation (from users)
5. Receive documentation updates (from users)

Figure 6.17 Library System application objectives.

6.4.2 Application Functions

We have defined the application context for both the Accounts Receivable and the Library Systems. We now define the application functions. We do this in four steps:

1. Define the "mainline" functional flow.
2. Define the scope.
3. Analyze the functional processes (i.e., the steps or subsystems).
4. Define the decision support functions.

6.4.2.1 Defining the mainline functional flow.   The entity diagrams gave us a static view of the system. In other words, we identified the interactions but did not define how one interaction related to another. We use the assembly line diagram to provide us with this dynamic view.

The *mainline* in a system links the principal processes together in a stream. We use the following procedure to develop the mainline:

1. In the application-level entity diagram, number the primary interactions (transactions) beginning with the transaction that starts the process.
2. Develop an assembly line for these transactions, beginning with the highest-number transaction on the right and working backward to the lowest.
3. Tick off the corresponding objectives as each transaction is added to the assembly line.
4. Group the remaining transactions in terms of like functions and draw concurrent (parallel) assembly lines for each group.
5. Enclose all the assembly lines in one brace to define the total system.

Returning to Figure 6.12, the application-level entity diagram for the Accounts Receivable System, we number the transactions beginning with the Order from the Customer and draw the corresponding assembly line diagram, Figure 6.18. We also tick off all our objectives in Figure 6.13. If our

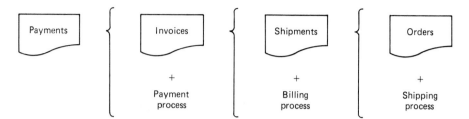

Figure 6.18 Accounts Receivable System: Mainline functional flow diagram.

Accounts Receivable System were more complex and we needed to produce a Customer Statement, our system would look like Figure 6.19. The corresponding application-level entity diagram showing the inclusion of the Customer Statement is illustrated in Figure 6.20. Our Accounts Receivable example has only one entity outside the application system. In real life, it is likely that there could be several outside entities (users).

For the Library System, returning to Figure 6.16, we number the primary transactions that are linked. These are Delivery Notice (Documenta-

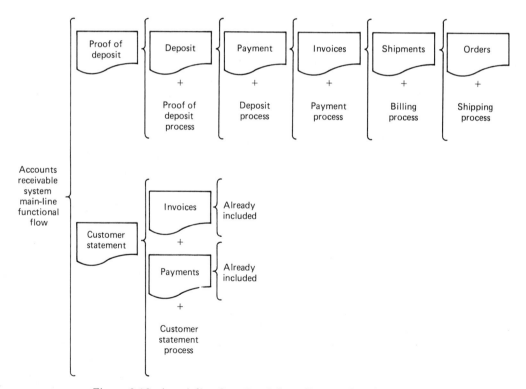

Figure 6.19 A mainline functional flow diagram showing concurrence.

ABC Company

Accounts receivable system

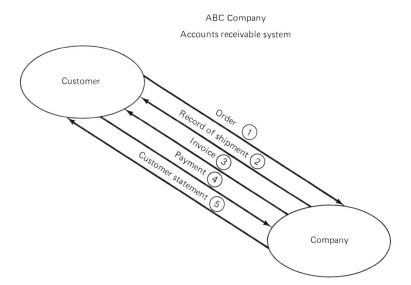

Figure 6.20 Application-level entity diagram showing the additional "Customer Statement" transaction.

tion), Charge-out Documentation, and Charge-in Documentation. We also know that a particular item of documentation after receipt could be charged out, updated, and obsoleted. All these can occur independent of the others. The mainline functional flow diagram for the Library System Documentation then has three parallel assembly lines, as shown in Figure 6.21. With this diagram completed, we can tick off all our objectives in Figure 6.17.

The reader should note one major difference between the Accounts Receivable System in Figure 6.19 and the Library System in Figure 6.21. The outputs in Figure 6.19 are documents, while the outputs in Figure 6.21 are records. This is because the Library System is a control system and except for the Delivery Notice and the Obsoletion Notice, which originate from the user, there is no movement of paper between the library and the user. (The Library Documentation is paper but is not part of the control system.)

Further, in Figure 6.16, the Library System application-level entity diagram, the first transaction is the Delivery Notice from the user to the library. The second transaction is the Charge-out of Documentation from the library to the user. In Figure 6.21, we note the insertion of the Documentation Record between the Delivery Notice and the Charge-out Record. The need for the Documentation Record became evident only when we were drawing the mainline functional flow diagram. This type of additional detail can be expected to occur as we define the functional flows. The entity diagrams provide us with only a limited view of the system.

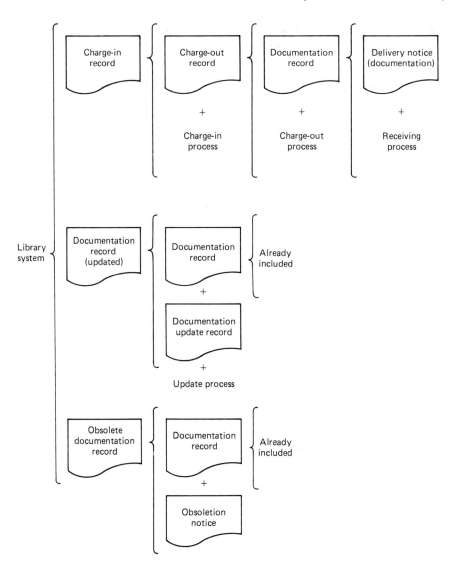

Figure 6.21 Library System: Mainline functional flow diagram.

6.4.2.2 Scope.   The mainline functional flow diagram gives us a complete overview of our system in terms of the inputs, outputs, processes, and concurrent assemblies. Because each process is separate from every other process, we can determine its time frame. Figure 6.22 shows the Accounts Receivable System as three subsystems: a Shipping Process, which occurs daily; a Billing Process, which occurs monthly; and a Payment Process, which also occurs monthly. In the Library System, the receiving and charging (loaning) of documentation is shown as three subsystems in Figure 6.23. All three occur at random.

Since we have divided the system into subsystems, we can now define the scope of our development. We can decide which subsystems we want to group and those we want to develop first, last, or not at all.

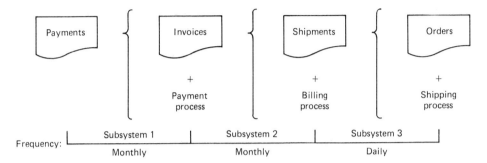

Figure 6.22 Accounts Receivable System: Functional processes.

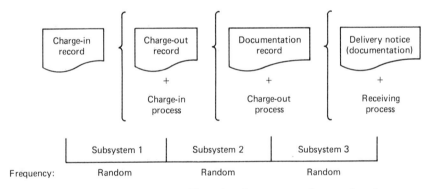

Figure 6.23 Library System: Functional processes for receive documentation and charge (loan) documentation.

6.4.2.3 Subsystem definition.

Each subsystem can now be decomposed into a series of tasks or procedures. At the lowest level, each task or procedure should produce either a single output or a set of related outputs. These lowest-level tasks or procedures should be defined as logical processes using Warnier-Orr diagrams based on the logical data structure of the output.

We saw an example of a process description in Figure 6.3. This process consists of several smaller processes or modules (as we have seen in earlier chapters). Each of these modules has a separate and distinct output. The outputs from Begin Order and Order Body are either new records or updated records in file. The output from Print Order is the printed Customer Order.

Dividing the process into two parts, the first part is a reflection of the data structure shown in Figure 6.2 in terms of the file update, while the second part is a reflection of the same data structure in terms of the production of the Customer Order form.

Let us decompose Subsystem 3 in Figure 6.23, the Documentation Receiving process. Here we have a different situation. Our case-study description in Chapter 2 tells us that when an item of Documentation is received, five records are set up:

1. The Daily Register
2. The On-Site Index
3. The Charge-out (Loan)
4. The History Log
5. The Document Processed Log

In the present manual system, identification data in these five records are duplicated. The present content of these records is listed in Table 4.5. They are reproduced below for convenience.

Daily Register

Document Number, Document Name, Document Volume Number, New/Update, Document Type (Documentation, Archival, etc.), Prepared By, Submitted By, Date Submitted

On-Site Index

Document Number, Document Name, Document Volume Number, Document Type (Documentation, Archival, etc.), Obsoletion Date, Date Filed, Filed By, Type of Access, Term of Loan

Document Processed Log

Document Number, Document Name, Volume Number, New/Update, Original/Photocopy, Date Processed

Charge-out Card

Document Number, Document Name, Volume Number, User Identification, Authorized By, Date Charged Out, Date Returned, Date Referenced

History Log

Document Number, Document Name, Volume Number, Date Updated

In each record, the Document Number, the Document Name, and the Volume Number are repeated. If we were to combine the five records into one, we could do this by initially establishing a Document record and then adding each of the other record's data to it as illustrated in Figure 6.24.

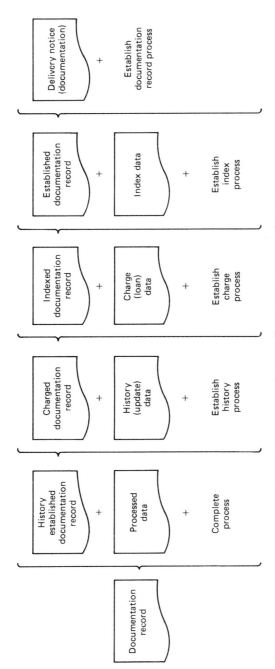

Figure 6.24 Library System: Receiving process subsystem.

The reasoning we have used in this subsystem so far should give us an insight into the type of system that we will require. This system will not consist of data flowing between the users and the library which is output on paper or on video screens. Instead, it will consist of a file or files being updated to maintain control over the documentation filed in the library.

The analyst is now faced with two choices: He can set up a procedure to establish and update a single Documentation record on receipt of new documentation, or he can put this information aside and proceed with the analysis of the rest of the system and finally build a logical data structure for the total system. If he chooses the latter, he can establish processes to establish, update, and delete records based on this logical data structure. He can also identify management reports and build procedures to provide these reports. We cover the handling of these reports in the next section.

The particular Library subsystem that we have just reviewed has a logical record as an output. Generally, the analyst could expect to develop a functional flow diagram in which a physical output (e.g., a report, a screen, or an invoice) from one process is input into the next process in the chain.

6.4.2.4 Decision support functions. Systems are built to serve three basic management needs. These are the need to operate, the need to control, and the need to make decisions. Operational information is generally specific and does not change much unless basic functions change. Outputs are well defined. Control information is less specific but can most often be specified and outputs defined. Decision-making information is based on "what if?" types of questions being asked. So outputs are not specific and have to be answered from the information in file. The most effective tools to extract this type of information are query languages and/or decision-support software. The use of these languages and software is simplified if the files are structured so that the typical search keys are easily accessed.

In Section 6.4.2.3, we concluded that we needed a logical data structure to meet the operating needs of the Library System. But we did not discuss how we would do this. The subject of logical data-base design is discussed at length in Chapter 4. Orr does not discuss this subject in *Structured Requirements Definition* [2] except to state that "Structured Systems Development now includes a data-base design process that produces what we call *logical bases files*. The logical bases files mirror the requirements view by dividing the data base into entities, transactions, and cycles/events. Logical keys are placed on files so the transaction bases files can be selected, sorted, and merged to provide different views of the data."

The statement above can be interpreted differently by different readers. Only those who have been taught the process by Ken Orr and Associates, Inc., know how to apply it. My interpretation is that logical data structures are built to meet the specific needs of each operational and known control output. These logical data structures can be either flat files or hierarchical files. Each of these files is independent. The files are linked by grouping them through tables in terms of entities (users), transactions, and cycles/ events. This enables a particular file to be accessed in terms of an entity (user), a type of transaction, or a time frame (random, daily, weekly, etc.). The known planning search keys are inserted in the files as data elements. Data can be accessed through the table groupings, the search keys, or a combination of the table groupings and the search keys.

In principle, the approach outlined above may appear to be simple. In reality, it is likely that there would be considerable detail in the process which the reader would require if he were to apply it correctly. If the reader wished to use Orr's logical data-base design technique, he would be advised to invest in the cost of having at least one person taught by Ken Orr and Associates, Inc.

6.4.3 Application Results (Principal Outputs)

The definition of the application results is done in three steps:

1. Identify the principal outputs.
2. Define the principal outputs.
3. Define the organizational cycles.

6.4.3.1 Principal outputs identification. The principal outputs of a system provide the data needed to meet the system's functions. These outputs include management reports, checks, invoices, video screens, and files needed to interface with other systems. A system can also have secondary outputs which aid in the capturing of data and the running of the system. Examples include input screens, control reports, and edit listings. Here we are concerned only with the primary outputs. The secondary outputs are identified and defined during the development of the physical solutions.

The tool used to identify the principal outputs is the *in-out diagram*. This is a Warnier-Orr diagram which lists the inputs and the outputs. Figure 6.25 is an example of an in-out diagram for the billing process in the Accounts Receivable System extracted from Figure 6.18. The additional inputs and outputs shown in Figure 6.25 would have been identified during the billing process subsystem definition.

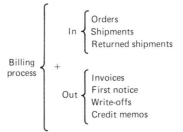

Figure 6.25 Accounts Receivable System: In-out diagram for the billing process.

6.4.3.2 Principal outputs definition.   Each principal output is defined as follows:

1. Define the logical data layout of the form.
2. Provide a sample or a simulation of the form.
3. Define the logical output structure with a Warnier-Orr diagram.
4. Define the data elements in a data dictionary.

Figure 6.26 is an example of the logical data layout of an invoice. Each variable on the form is identified by a "bucket" drawn under it. Figure 6.27 is a sample of the same invoice with data values included. The logical output structure for the invoice is shown in Figure 6.28.

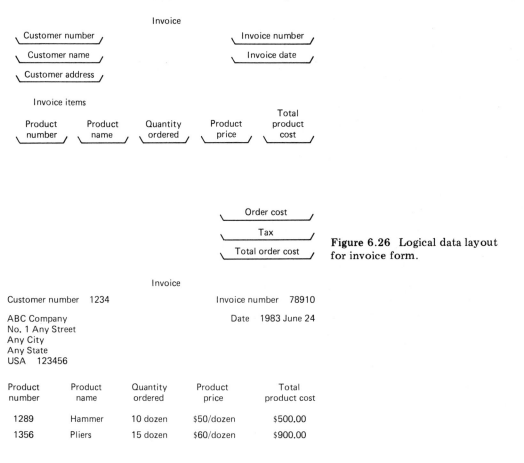

Figure 6.26 Logical data layout for invoice form.

Figure 6.27 Sample output for invoice.

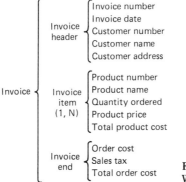

Figure 6.28 Output structure Warnier-Orr diagram.

Each data element is entered in a data dictionary and defined as follows:

- Data element name
- Data element identification
- Type
- Description
- Synonyms
- Where used
- Computation/decision logic

6.4.3.3 Organizational cycles. All systems that are either completely or partially batch are cyclical. In other words, the outputs are produced in cycles at different times to meet different needs. Figure 6.29 lists the outputs and their frequencies for the Accounts Receivable System. These data can be converted into a Warnier-Orr diagram showing the different time frames (cycles) for each output in the system. Orr refers to this as a system diagram (Figure 6.30).

Output	Frequency
Orders	100/day
Shipments	500/week
Invoices	50/week
Payments	10/day
Deposits	0–1/day
Proof of deposit	0–1/day
Customer statements	100/month

Figure 6.29 Accounts receivable diagram outputs and frequencies.

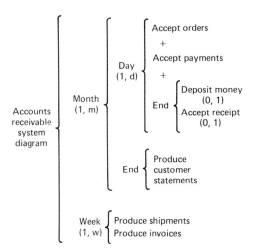

Figure 6.30 Accounts Receivable System diagram.

6.5 PHYSICAL DEFINITION PHASE

The logical definition of the system provides a detailed requirement of what the system must do. In the physical definition, we convert the logical definition into a physical specification of how the system will be built. We do this in five steps:

1. Define the constraints on building the system.
2. Define alternative physical solutions.
3. Define the benefits and the risks for each alternative solution.
4. Select a solution.
5. Prepare the final requirements definition document.

6.5.1 Constraints

The *constraints* are limitations on building the system. Generally, the two biggest constraints are computer processing capacity and storage capacity. For example, insufficient processing capacity can cause totally unacceptable response times in interactive, on-line systems. Insufficient disk space could eliminate an on-line system. Reliability and security could influence the physical design if proper security software is not available. The availability of a data-base management system could dictate the use of hierarchical, network, or relational file structures. The first step, then, is to identify the constraints on building the system as specified in the logical definition.

6.5.2 Alternative Physical Solutions

Several different physical solutions should be considered, including "doing nothing" and buying a software package from a vendor. If the latter is considered, it is essential that the logical definition be done and the selection be made based on the requirements identified. Often, organizations have a general idea of their needs and search the market for a suitable package. The package that is chosen with a limited set of requirements specified could be the most popular package in the market or the one with the best sales personnel. Unfortunately, it may not meet the organization's real needs and the cost of modification of the package and subsequent modification of the updates could far exceed the anticipated savings over building a system in-house.

6.5.3 Benefits and Risks

Most managers are familiar with cost/benefit analysis. But many managers tend to forget what risks can play a key role in their decision making. Two types of risks, in particular, should be considered. These are: gambling on a new technological breakthrough and the impact the delay or failure of the new system could have on the organization, and the effect that not building the system now or at all could have on the organization later. An example of the latter could be a small airline which does not require an on-line reservation system today, but could not compete without one if it expanded its operations later.

6.5.4 Recommended Course of Action

Selecting the particular solution is a management prerogative. This does not release the analyst from his responsibility to guide management in its choice. When the recommendations are made to management, they should be accompanied by a *weighting chart* so that each solution can be compared in terms of each weighting factor. This gives management a better perspective of the choices available and the option of selecting a solution which may not be the one with the highest score.

6.5.5 Final Requirements Definition Document

The final task in structured requirements definition is to compile a report consolidating the material produced. Orr suggests Figure 6.31 as a suitable table of contents for this report.

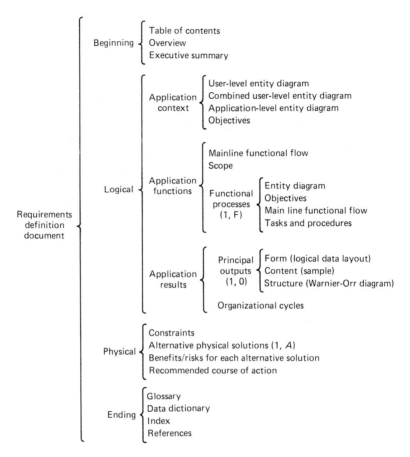

Figure 6.31 Requirements definition document: Table of contents.

6.6 STRUCTURED REQUIREMENTS DEFINITION
PROCESS DIAGRAM

The steps followed in structured requirements definition can be put on a
Warnier-Orr diagram. Figure 6.32 shows the phases and the steps as a hierarchy. Figure 6.33 shows the flow of information and how the different
pieces of documentation in the logical design phase fit together. Figures 6.32
and 6.33, together, serve as an effective checklist for the structured requirements definition process.

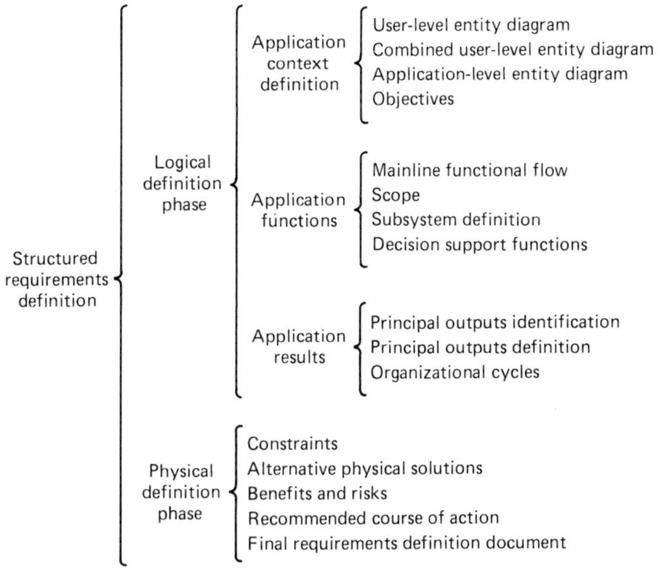

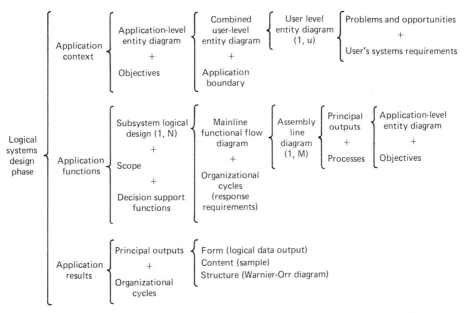

Figure 6.32 Structured requirements definition process drawn as a Warnier-Orr diagram.

Figure 6.33 Logical systems design phase redrawn to show the flow of information.

6.7 STRUCTURE CLASH

Structured requirements definition is based on the definition of outputs which best meet the system's objectives. We saw in Section 6.4.2.3 that each subsystem is decomposed into logical processes which are structured hierarchically according to the hierarchical structure of the output being produced. An "ordering" structure clash occurs when the output has a different hierarchy from the input. Figure 6.34 illustrates this situation for a Documentation Update record. The logical record is sequenced by Update Serial Number within Documentation Identification Number. The required report is sequenced by the Date Filed by Date Received by the person it is prepared by.

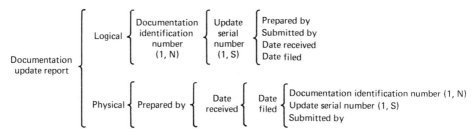

Figure 6.34 Example of an "Ordering Clash" between a logical record and a physical report.

Two solutions can be used to overcome this problem. The easier solution is to sort the input records into the output sequence using an intermediate work file. This solution entails the need for two programs and the use of the work file. The second solution is to use "inversion" or flattening of one program and to make it a subroutine of the second. This solution requires sufficient work space or on-line storage to store the complete file.

How does inversion function? First, a table is set up to match the hierarchy of the output required. In our example, this is the required format of the Documentation Update report. Each record that is input is changed by the subroutine into the output format and entered in the table in the sequence of the output report. The print program then prints the required output.

6.8 OTHER APPLICATIONS OF THE CASE STUDY

The discussion of the case study in this chapter has been restricted to the system documentation. If the reader intends to use the structured requirements definition techniques, he may find it worthwhile to apply the principles to another area from the case study, for example the Archival Documents, before he puts his knowledge to use.

6.9 ADVANTAGES AND DISADVANTAGES OF STRUCTURED REQUIREMENTS DEFINITION

Advantages

1. The primary advantage of structured requirements definition is that it results in systems which are a direct reflection of the outputs, since it is the outputs that provide the user with the data he needs in order to function.
2. The hierarchical design structure, followed in the functional flow (assembly line) diagrams, ensures that the logical subsystem design and the decomposition of the subsystems into processes satisfy the time frames of the outputs.
3. The use of the Warnier-Orr diagram ensures a one-parent-to-many-children relationship, which, in turn ensures the production of single outputs from multiple inputs.

Disadvantages

1. Emphasis on the outputs and their content tends to result in a system with multiple files in which considerable duplication of data could occur. Mention is made by Orr [2] of the development of "logical bases files," but no explanation is given of how to build them. Further, they are discussed only in the context of decision support and so are likely to be missed completely by the reader.
2. The Library System case study highlights a problem in the technique which I attempted to resolve in this chapter. Orr [2] does not discuss the design of systems where the requirement is for a logical data base which is constantly interactively updated and does not involve "to-and-fro" movement of information between entities (users). An example is the establishment and updating of the Documentation record as and when different actions (registration, charging, updating, etc.) occur. The only required outputs from this system which are user readable are views of the records in the data base used by the librarians for information and update, the control reports, and the occasional planning reports. The control reports are produced at regular intervals, but they only extract snapshots of the data stored in the data base at these points in time. The approach taken in this chapter to overcome this problem was that each logical record in the data base was an "output." This enabled the system to be defined.

REFERENCES

1. Kenneth T. Orr, *Structured Systems Development*, Yourdon Press, New York, 1977.
2. Kenneth T. Orr, *Structured Requirements Definition*, Ken Orr and Associates, Inc., Topeka, KS, 1981.

7

Jackson System Development

7.1 WHAT IS JSD?

Jackson system development (JSD) is described by Michael Jackson [1] as "a method for specifying and implementing computer systems. These activities include requirements specification, functional specification, logical system design, application system design, physical system design, program specification and design, program implementation, and system and program maintenance." In short, JSD covers every aspect of system design and development. JSD is done over six steps. The first four are concerned with specification, the fifth and sixth with implementing the specification.

To quote Jackson: "A JSD system may be regarded as a simulation of the relevant parts of the real world outside the system; system functions are regarded as providing outputs derived from the behaviour of this simulation." The emphasis is on the "real world outside the system which is dynamic, with events occurring in time ordered sequence." The JSD model simulates the real world and in the process conveys the scope of the system to the user in clear terms. The user then has the opportunity to add, delete, or modify this scope. The system functions are added to the model and provide the required outputs. In the implementation of a system, timing is paramount (e.g., the outputs could be required at random, daily, weekly, and so on). This timing is taken into account and the system is implemented. The implementation could be on a single processor or on multiple processors; could include external schedulers, single programs with subroutines, multiple programs; and so on.

JSD is iterative and it is expected that elaboration of detail during the various steps brings to light entities and actions not identified at the beginning. (Entities here are part of the real world outside the computer system and perform actions or have actions performed on them in a set order.)

Students of Jackson system programming (JSP; see Jackson's *Principles of Program Design* [2]) will be familiar with the thoroughness and elegance of Jackson's work. These same qualities are evident in JSD. Jackson's techniques ensure that not only are the user's needs clearly specified, but the systems respond to change and are easily maintained. The comprehensive detail of the development and implementation process has a price tag attached to it. This is the diffusion of JSP throughout the process. This is most evident in the implementation steps. However, the earlier steps of JSD are concerned with the identification of structure clashes in the description of the real-world subject matter, and structure text at the programming level is used throughout the process.

Other techniques described earlier have been taken to the level where the reader can apply at least the basics to design and develop computer systems. JSD cannot be summarized in the same manner, no more than a graduate-level text on calculus can be summarized in a single chapter. Instead, JSD will be described using the Library System to explain to the reader what JSD is and to give him a flavor for how it is applied. The term *structure clash* was explained in Section 6.7 in terms of "ordering." Two other types of structure clash are also discussed in this chapter, as they are pertinent to the application of JSD.

7.1.1 Static and Dynamic Models

A static model presents a snapshot at a point in time. An example of a snapshot is data in a data base between updates. A dynamic model illustrates a flow of data. An example of dynamic data is the text of this chapter being input to a microcomputer. Every system has both dynamic and static components. System design techniques sometimes emphasize one or the other. In JSD, the emphasis is on modeling the dynamic component. In fact, Jackson does not discuss the design of data bases except as a fallout from the implementation steps.

In Chapter 6 the term *concurrency*, meaning parallelism or multitasking, was used (Sections 6.2.4 and 6.4.2.1). In JSD, Jackson states that all processes are sequential. They are sequential because only one thing can happen at one time in one process. Many processes can occur simultaneously within a system without infringing this rule. This simultaneous occurrence of processes is what Orr refers to as concurrency. So, in fact, they are describing the same situation from two different viewpoints.

7.2 DEVELOPMENT STEPS

JSD consists of six development steps:

1. Entity action step
2. Entity structure step
3. Initial model step
4. Function step
5. System timing step
6. Implementation step

7.2.1 Entity Action Step

In this step the real-world entities and the actions they perform or suffer are described.

What is an entity? An entity in JSD is not the entity commonly found in a file or data base. An entity in a file or data base is generally a logical record which has keys and attributes. A *JSD entity* must exist as part of the real world outside the system; it must perform or suffer actions in a time ordering; it must be capable of being regarded as an individual or an individual type and of being uniquely named; and the system must be required to produce or use information about it. Examples of entities are: Customer, Account, Part, Widget No. 3456, and Employee. Examples of items which are not entities include: Error Report, Date, and Age. Error Report is a system output; Date and Age do not perform or suffer actions.

What is an action? An action must take place at a point in time; it cannot be extended over a period of time. "To live" is not an action; "to kill" is an action. An action must take place in the real world outside the system. "Issue error report" is not an action. An action cannot be a composite. "Issue a journal entry" involves a debit and a credit and is therefore not an action.

In the Library System, the following are entities:

- User
- Archival Document Off-Site
- Documentation On-Site Volume
- Documentation Off-Site Volume
- Obsolete Documentation Off-Site Volume
- Documentation On-Site Update
- Documentation Off-Site Update

These are entities because they are all physical items outside the computer system. They all suffer actions in a time ordering and can be individually named. System Documentation (i.e., documentation associated with a particular system) is not a JSD entity because it can consist of several volumes and updates, each of which can be identified separately. In fact, five of the seven JSD entities named above are part of System Documentation.

The actions performed or suffered by the Library System JSD entities are:

Entity: User
Actions: Charge Out, Return, Reference

Entity: Archival Document Off-Site
Actions: Register, Ship Off-Site, File, Retrieve from Off-Site, Charge Out, Return, Reference, Reship Off-Site, Make Obsolete, Discard

Entity: Documentation On-Site Volume
Actions: Register, Copy, File, Charge Out, Return, Reference

Entity: Documentation Off-Site Volume
Actions: Ship Off-Site, File, Retrieve from Off-Site, Charge Out, Return, Reference, Reship Off-Site

Entity: Obsolete Documentation Off-Site Volume
Actions: Make Obsolete, Ship Off-Site, File, Retrieve from Off-Site, Charge Out, Return, Reference, Reship Off-Site, Discard

Entity: Documentation On-Site Update
Actions: Register, Copy, File

Entity: Documentation Off-Site Update
Actions: Ship Off-Site, File

Actions are described, linked to the entities, and given attributes. (In every other technique we have examined, attributes or data elements are part of records. Attributes are linked to actions in JSD because the action changes the value of the attribute.)

Register: Establish a record of the document. Action of Archival Document Off-Site, Documentation On-Site Volume, Documentation Update On-Site.
    Attributes: Document Identification, Author, Document Date, Date Registered, Type of Access, Submitted By, Term of Loan.

Copy: Make a copy of the document. Action of Documentation On-Site, Documentation On-Site Update.
    Attributes: Date Copied, Copied By.

File: Place document in storage cabinet in proper place. Action of Archival Document Off-Site, Documentation On-Site Volume, Documentation Off-Site Volume, Obsolete Documentation Volume, Documentation On-Site Update, Documentation Off-Site Update.

Attributes: Filed By, Date Filed, Location.

Charge Out: Loan document and record the loan. Action of Archival Document Off-Site, Documentation On-Site Volume, Documentation Off-Site Volume, Obsolete Documentation Volume, User.

Attributes: Userid, Date Charged Out, Authorization.

Return: Return the document and record the return. Action of Archival Document Off-Site, Documentation On-Site Volume, Documentation Off-Site Volume, Obsolete Documentation Volume, User.

Attributes: Userid, Date Returned.

Reference: Reference the document and record the reference. Action of Archival Document Off-Site, Documentation On-Site Volume, Documentation Off-Site Volume, Obsolete Documentation Volume, User.

Attributes: Userid, Date Referenced, Authorization

Ship Off-Site: Ship the document off-site. Action of Archival Document Off-Site, Documentation Off-Site Volume, Obsolete Documentation Volume, Documentation Update Off-Site.

Attributes: Date Shipped Off-Site.

Retrieve from Off-Site: Bring back the document from off-site. Action of Archival Document Off-Site, Documentation Off-Site Volume, Obsolete Documentation Volume.

Attributes: Date Retrieved from Off-Site.

Discard: Discard the document. Action of Archival Document Off-Site, Obsolete Documentation Volume.

Attributes: Discarded By, Date Discarded.

Make Obsolete: Change status of document to obsolete. Action of Obsolete Documentation Volume, Archival Documentation Off-Site.

Attributes: Date Obsoleted, Obsoleted By.

7.2.2 Entity Structure Step

JSD models the real-world entity for its entire lifetime. For example, a model of a customer's bank account would illustrate the opening of the account; all the possible transactions that could occur in it, such as deposits, withdrawals, interest payments, and service charges; and finally the termination of the account. The model assumes that this account is processed on a single processor solely at the disposal of the particular account. So if the processor is programmed to react to the actions identified during the lifetime of the account, you can expect it to be idle most of the time but to carry on executing instructions exactly at the point where it left off when a new transaction occurs. If systems were built like this in real life, one could expect large numbers of microprocessors to be set up to meet the needs of the millions of bank customers. This is neither practical nor possible. In JSD, during the implementation steps, the individual processors are replaced by mainframe computers, and the individual local or internal variables (attribute values) for each process are replaced by files and data bases.

In the entity structure step, we construct an abstract model of the real world. This abstract model will display the entities and the actions defined in the entity action step. The tool used to diagram this abstraction is the structure diagram.

7.2.2.1 Structure diagram. Because the actions of entities are ordered in time, the model must clearly display this time ordering. Figure 7.1 is an illus-

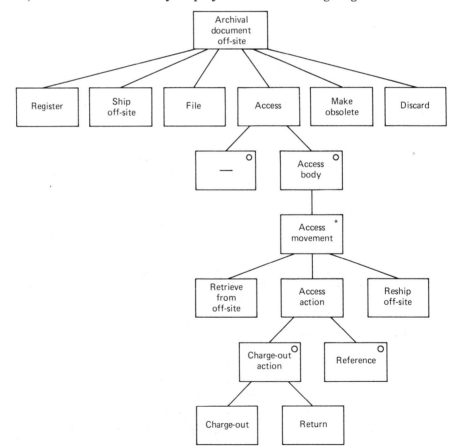

Figure 7.1 Archival document off-site entity structure diagram.

tration of a structure diagram for the Archival Document Off-Site entity. Structure diagrams illustrate the three basic constructs (i.e., sequence, iteration, and selection). Structure diagrams are trees. The topmost box is called the *root* and the boxes with no further connections below them are called *leaves.* Boxes can be parents or children. Any parent can have one or more children but no child can have more than one parent. Structure charts, discussed in Chapter 5, which show "fan in" would not satisfy this rule.

> *Sequence:* A sequence is indicated by leaving the child boxes unmarked. In Figure 7.1, Archival Documents Off-Site is a sequence. The meaning of sequence is that for each instance of the parent, each child is executed once, beginning from the leftmost and proceeding to the rightmost. So Register occurs once, Ship Off-Site occurs once, and so on, until Discard occurs once.

> *Iteration:* An iteration is indicated by placing an asterisk in the top right-hand corner of the child box. Each iteration can have only one child. Access Body is an example of iteration and its child is Access Movement. The meaning of iteration is that for each instance of Access Body, Access Movement can occur zero or more times.

> *Selection:* A selection is indicated by marking each child of a selection with a small circle in the top right-hand corner. A selection can have two or more children. The meaning of selection is that for each instance of the selection box, one instance of a child occurs. So, for each instance of Access, Null or Access Body occurs. The Null box shown with a "–" means that "nothing" occurs.

The reader should note that the constructs are indicated by notation in the child boxes and not in the parent boxes. Figures 7.1 to 7.7 illustrate the

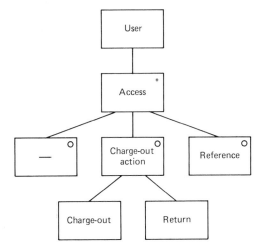

Figure 7.2 User entity structure diagram.

structure diagrams for the Library System's entities and actions modeling the real world. Let us examine the Archival Document Off-Site Diagram (Figure 7.1).

The Archival Document Off-Site process is a sequence in which the document is registered in the library, shipped off-site, and filed. If the document is requested, it is brought back from off-site storage and then either charged out to a user or the user is permitted to reference it in the library. It is possible that the document may never be requested during its lifetime. It is also possible that it may be requested many times. A further possibility is that the user who requests the document could change his mind after he asks for it and before it is retrieved. The document is made obsolete and finally discarded. This possible sequence of events is shown in the structure diagram.

The Archival Document Off-Site box is a sequence. So its children Register, Ship Off-Site, File, Access, Make Obsolete, and Discard occur in sequence. The box Access is a selection and has two possibilities: Either the document may never be requested, the Null box, or it could be requested,

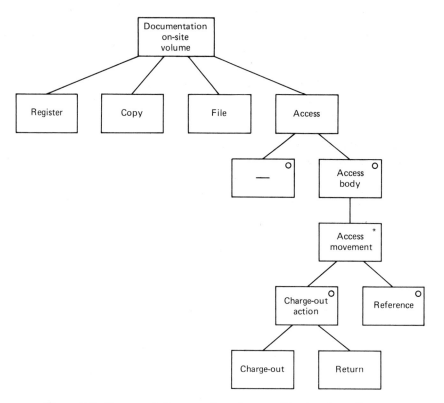

Figure 7.3 Documentation on-site volume entity structure diagram.

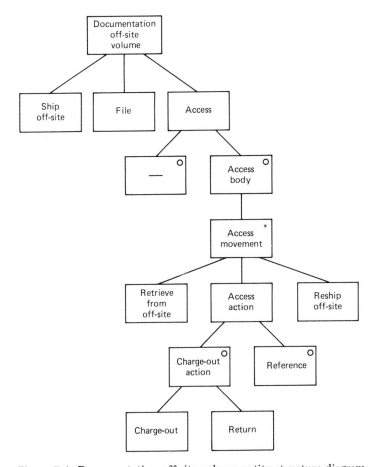

Figure 7.4 Documentation off-site volume entity structure diagram.

the Access Body box. The Access Body box is an iteration and has only one child, Access Movement. This iteration implies that the document could be requested and the request canceled before the document is retrieved, or the document could be retrieved once or many times. The box Access Movement is a sequence and its children are Retrieve from Off-Site, Access Action, and Reship Off-Site. The box Access Action is a selection and has two children, Charge-out Action and Reference. This means that the document can be borrowed or referenced. The box Charge-out Action is a sequence with children Charge-out and Return (i.e., once borrowed, the document must be returned).

Figure 7.1 reflects the real world of the Archival Document Off-Site. The reader might now ask if it is comprehensive enough. For example, what happens if the user loses the document? There are probably many such situations that could be identified. But the identification of the entities, actions, and attributes and the drawing of the structure diagram clearly limit the scope of the computer system to be designed, and this is done with the knowledge and consent of the system's owner.

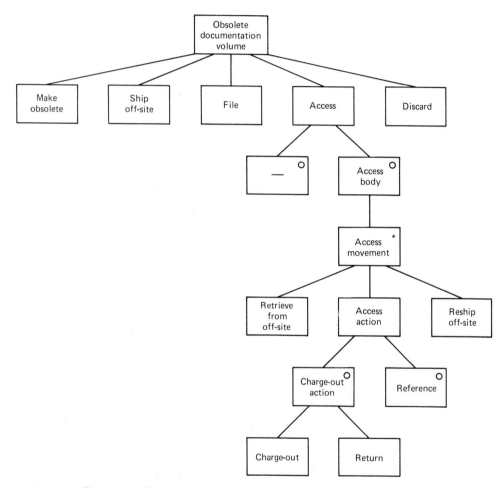

Figure 7.5 Obsolete documentation volume entity structure diagram.

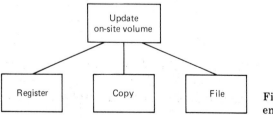

Figure 7.6 Update on-site volume entity structure diagram.

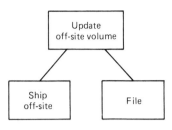

Figure 7.7 Update off-site volume entity structure diagram.

7.2.3 Initial Model Step

Sections 7.2.1 and 7.2.2 (Steps 1 and 2) have given us an abstract description of the real world in terms of sequential processes. In the initial model step, the developer specifies the system to be built by specifying a simulation of the real world. This is done by creating a model which will reflect the abstraction of the real world (i.e., for each real-world process there will be a corresponding process in the model). The first task in this step is to state how the real-world process is to be connected to the model process.

Before we proceed further, the reader should become more acquainted with some of the terms used in JSD. They will become clearer as they are used.

7.2.3.1 JSD terms

Local variable: the value of an attribute at any point in a program's execution: for example, the value of the attribute Balance when a customer makes a deposit.

State vector: the set of all the local variables in a particular process.

Data-stream connection: a stream of sequential messages, such as this text being keyed into a microcomputer, and connects two processes.

State-vector connection: used when one process inspects the state vector of another process. This is similar to taking a snapshot of the variables' values at a point in time.

Text pointer: the special variable in a process which indicates where the last instruction was executed in the program. The program will begin execution when instructed from this point. To ensure that meaningless data are not obtained when the local variables are read, the text pointer is set up to be read only before a Read or after a Write instruction. An example of this type of variable is "Registered" in the action Register. Its values would be "yes" or "no."

7.2.3.2 System specification diagram.

The *system specification diagram* or SSD is used to represent the connection between the real world and the model. Figure 7.8 shows examples of SSDs. The suffix "−0" after the en-

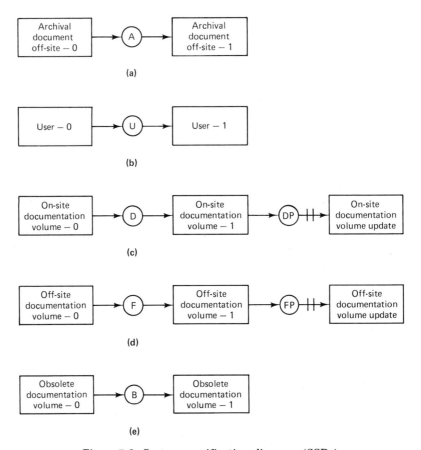

Figure 7.8 System specification diagrams (SSDs).

tity indicates a real-world process, while the suffix "−1" indicates a model process.

Two types of connection are used between processes. These are data stream and state vector. The most common type of connection is by data stream, in which a stream of messages is sent from the real world to the model process. A data stream is drawn as a circle. In Figure 7.8, A, U, D, F, and B are data streams. A state-vector connection is used when a reading is needed of the state variables in a process in a point in time. An example would be a report listing all the Archival Documents charged out until a particular date. A state-vector connection is drawn as a diamond. (In Figure 7.9, CH is a state-vector connection.)

The connection may be 1:1, 1:M (many), or M:N (many to many). For example, in Figure 7.8(c), process On-Site Documentation Volume−1 occurs once and process On-Site Documentation Update can occur zero or many times. The two vertical bars indicate the "many" situation.

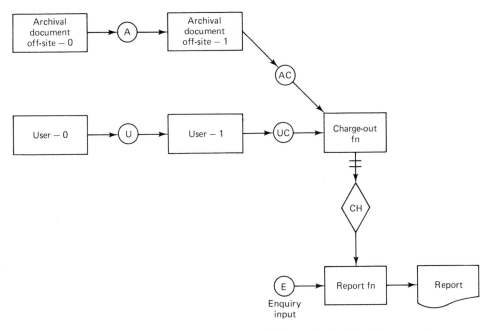

Figure 7.9 Function "Provide a List of Users by Archival Document
· Off-Site Charged Out."

7.2.3.3 Structure text.   The following notation is limited to the use of
structure text in the examples. Should the reader require information on the
complete text used in JSD, he should refer to the two Jackson textbooks discussed earlier [1, 2].

Sequence	Selection	Iteration
A seq	A sel (cond-B)	A itr while (cond-B)
B;	B;	B;
C;	A alt (cond-C)	A end
D;	C;	
A end	A alt (cond-D)	
	D;	
	A end	

Sequence: In the A sequence, action B occurs first and is followed by
actions C and D.

Selection: In the A selection, a particular condition indicates action B,
a second condition action C, and a third condition action D.

Iteration: In the A iteration, action B is repeated as long as a particular
condition exists.

In the entity structure step, we drew a structure diagram of the real world of the Archival Document Off-Site (Figure 7.1). Assuming that the model duplicates the real world, the structure text using JSD notation for Archival Document Off-Site—1 would be

```
Archival Document Off-Site—1 seq.
    read A;
    Register; read A;
    Ship Off-Site; read A;
    File; read A;
    Access sel (Null)
        Null; read A;
    Access alt (Access Body)
        Access Body itr while (Access Movement)
            Access Movement seq
                Retrieve from Off-Site; read A;
                Access Action sel (Charge-out Action)
                    Charge-out Action seq
                        Charge-out; read A;
                            Return; read A;
                    Charge-out Action end
                    Reference; read A;
                Access Action end
                Reship Off-Site; read A;
            Access Movement end
        Access Body end
    Access end
    Make Obsolete; read A;
    Discard;
Archival Document Off-Site end
```

The reader should match the structure text to the structure diagram. He will find that the text exactly follows the sequence in the diagram. The only added information is the "read" of the data stream. This "read" follows the "read ahead" rule, so that the model accesses the data before it reacts to them.

In the initial model step, a computer model has been specified which simulates the real world. In the next step, we add "function" to the model to meet specific output requirements. By separating function from the real-world simulation, we can supply any required information by adding processes to the basic model.

In the simple situation described above, it was assumed that there would be no problem with the input to the system. In reality, all kinds of things can go wrong or not be feasible. To overcome these errors, an input subsystem must generally be built to ensure that the data fed to the model are clean and acceptable.

7.2.4 Function Step

In the function step, the developer specifies the system functions in terms of the model. In other words, the model is extended to provide required outputs. This is done by specifying the event or combination of events that occur in the real world that trigger the production of such and such outputs, and incorporating these events in the model. Structure text is then written for the detailed specifications of the functions.

Let us suppose that we have been asked to produce a list of Archival Documents Off-Site charged out, together with the names of the users who borrowed them. Figure 7.9 is an SSD illustrating this function. The diagram combines the SSDs for the Archival Document Off-Site and User entities and adds a Charge-out process. Input to the Charge-out process is by two data streams which are merged. The report we require is produced by the Report Function process, which obtains the charge-out data from the Charge-out process by state-vector connection. The structure text for the four model processes follows:

```
Archival Document Off-Site—1
    Access Body itr while (Access Movement)
        Access Movement seq
            Retrieve from Off-Site; read A;
            Access Action sel (Charge-out Action)
                Charge-out Action seq
                    Charge-out; write Archivaldocid to
                        Charge-out fn; read A;
                    Return; read A;
                Charge-out Action end
                Reference; read A;
            Access Action end
            Reship Off-Site; read A;
        Access Movement end
    Access Body end


User-1
    User-1 itr while (Access)
        read U;
        Access sel (Null)
            Null; read U;
        Access alt (Charge-out Action)
            Charge-out Action seq
                Charge-out; write Userid to Charge-out fn;
                    read U;
                Return; read U;
            Charge-out Action end
```

```
        Access alt (Reference)
            Reference;
        Access end
    User-1 end


Charge-out fn process
    Charge-out seq
        read Archivaldocid and Userid;
        Charge-out; read Archivaldocid and Userid;
        Return;
    Charge-out end


Enquiry process
    Enquiry fn seq
        read Enquiry Input;
        Enquiry fn Body itr
            Enquiry seq
                get state vector of Charge-out fn
                write Archivaldicid, Userid;
            Enquiry end
            read Enquiry Input;
        Enquiry fn Body end
    Enquiry fn end
```

In Figure 7.9 we have two data streams, AC and UC, merging together and being input to the Charge-out fn process. These two streams merge together without any structure clash, as a Charge-out always precedes a Return in both the Archival Document Off-Site-1 and the User-1 processes. (Structure clash is discussed in Section 7.3.)

7.2.5 System Timing Step

So far, JSD has not considered timing in any of the system processes. Timing is affected when information is needed, which in turn affects when the processes are run. If information is needed instantaneously, the process will be on-line in terms of update and enquiry. If the information is needed daily or weekly, the update may be on-line or batch, while the report process would probably be batch. Such timing constraints should not affect the SSD. A possible situation where the SSD could be affected would be where timing is built into the process, such as in a traffic light system where the lights in one direction change to red and the other set stays red for a couple of seconds. Another example could be where a count of transactions on a computerized teller is recorded on the hour to establish a history of peaks and valleys. Where the SSD is not affected, the timing constraints are built into the system during the implementation step. In our example of the Archival Document Off-Site-User report, we will assume that the SSD is not affected by timing considerations.

7.2.6 System Implementation Step

The JSD specification defined in Sections 7.2.1 to 7.2.5 (Steps 1 to 5) is the specification of a process or a sequence of processes relating to a single entity or a single set of entities (e.g., a single Archival Document Off-Site, a single User, or a combination of the two). (In the preceding step we did examine an SSD to extract information about a series of Archival Documents Off-Site and a series of Users. Strictly speaking, this SSD related to only one Archival Document Off-Site and one User.) In the implementation step, we will describe how these single processes can be combined in real life.

The task faced by the developer during this implementation step is to identify how many real or virtual processors are to be used; where the number of processors is far smaller than the number of processes, how the processes will be distributed over the processors; and where one processor has to handle more than one process, how the time will be allocated to each. Added to this, the developer generally has to take into consideration factors such as the programming language to be used, a data-base management system, a data-base enquiry language, and a teleprocessing transaction monitor.

In our report example, the first task is to separate the common processes from the variables. By doing this, we now have the state vectors (records) separated from the processes and stored in files. The second task is to determine the number of processors to be used. We might use two processors, one for the Archival Document Off-Site-1 process, the User-1 process, and the Charge-out fn process; and one for the Report fn process. Or we might use a single processor for the whole system. The third task is to decide which processes require immediate execution and which can be delayed. This would indicate whether the processes should be on-line or batch.

Let us assume that we will use a single processor capable of handling all our needs. We will also assume that all the processes are to be run as a single task under the control of a scheduler, and that the report information will be printed out as it is produced.

Figure 7.10 is the system implementation diagram (SID) for the report system. The system has two master files, the Archival Document Off-Site file and the User file. The four processes are converted to subroutines and brought under the control of a single scheduling process. This scheduler is a new program that we have not specified. This scheduling program reads all the input and writes all the output. It calls each subroutine in turn and has access to the master files.

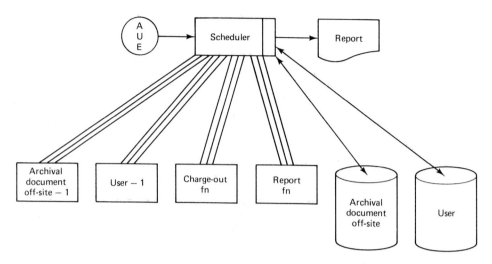

Figure 7.10 System implementation diagram: Version 1.

Another implementation could be to replace the scheduler with one of the processes and use the remaining processes as subroutines. Figure 7.11 illustrates this implementation.

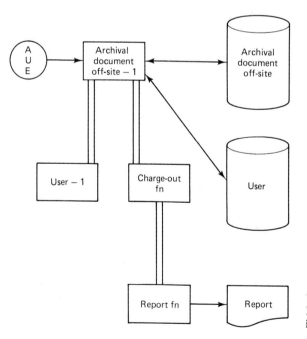

Figure 7.11 System implementation diagram: Version 2.

7.3 STRUCTURE CLASH

Two or more data streams which merge as input to a process, or are output from a process, may not have the same data structure or be in the same sequence. Jackson refers to these structure conflicts as *structure clashes* and divides them into three classes: boundary, ordering, and interleaving. The usual approach to solving these structure conflicts is to execute file sorts and additional programs. Jackson solves these conflicts through the use of subroutines, tables in primary storage or on-line files, and processes that reflect the data structures.

7.3.1 Boundary Clash

A *boundary clash* occurs when the data input to a process have a different boundary from the data output and are in the same sequence. A simple example is an 80-column card file containing the contents of this chapter. The first 15 characters of each card are reserved for control data and the remaining 65 characters contain the text. No two cards need contain the same number of words. This card file is input into a process which produces a report on the number of words in the text. Here the boundary for the input data is the 80-column card record. The boundary for the output is the report. This situation would normally require two independent programs, one to separate the words from the card record structure and the second to produce the report. Jackson converts one of these programs into a subroutine of the other and thereby reduces the processing.

7.3.2 Ordering Clash

An *ordering clash* occurs when the data input are in a different sequence from the data output. An illustration of this would be a table or matrix input by row into a process and a report produced on the information by column. Here, an intermediate sort prior to the report process would provide the input in the required output sequence. Jackson eliminates this sort by inverting one program and making it a subroutine of the second. Here sufficient primary storage would be required to hold the entire table before the new program incorporating the subroutine can provide the report or access to an on-line file would be necessary. (We discussed the ordering clash and inversion in Section 6.7.)

7.3.3 Interleaving Clash

An *interleaving clash* is also called a *multithreading clash*. It occurs when two or more data streams can contain the same data and the data can vary from transaction to transaction. This type of clash is more complex than the two described above. Consider the following example. A bank customer can have multiple accounts. At any point in time, he can open an account, deposit funds, withdraw funds, or close an account. These transactions can be carried out simultaneously so that more than one data stream is being input to the bank by the customer.

Jackson's solution to this problem would be to establish two separate processes, called Customer and Account, as illustrated in Figures 7.12 and 7.13. Merging data streams from these two processes presents no difficulty as the two processes have common actions, and data from only one Customer action can be merged with data from one Account action at one time.

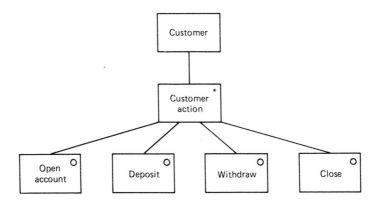

Figure 7.12 Customer entity structure diagram.

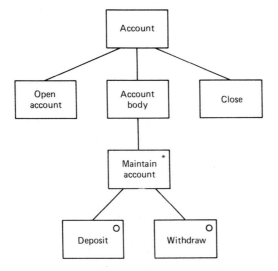

Figure 7.13 Account entity structure diagram.

7.4 NOT TOP-DOWN

Jackson is emphatic that JSD is not a top-down method for developing computer systems. The basic idea of top-down is stepwise refinement. The object to be developed is regarded as a hierarchy. The developer begins by stating the highest level of the hierarchy and decomposes this level into a number of smaller objects. This is continued until the lowest level has been reached. It is true that structure diagrams are hierarchies. But they are drawn only after the actions (the lowest level) have been defined in Step 1. System implementation diagrams (SIDs) are hierarchies. But these are drawn only in the last step and are dependent on the choice of process to be at the top. In one implementation, one process can be the scheduler and in another, a second process can take its place.

What is JSD, then? JSD can be considered a network which takes a series of sequential real-life and computer processes and through synthesis, builds them into a system. Further, these processes are defined using structure text even during the modeling of the real-world entities, and this ensures that the specification can be programmed.

7.5 ADVANTAGES AND DISADVANTAGES OF JSD

Advantages

1. JSD is particularly suited to the development of systems with a strong time dimension and in which the process produces the output on its own. Examples of such systems are operating systems, program generators, compilers, elevator systems, and missile guidance systems.
2. JSD can also be used to develop any form of business system.

Disadvantages

1. JSD is a very detailed and comprehensive development tool. It takes a very competent person to use it effectively and it can also consume large amounts of development time. This time is a very valuable quantity and most organizations will settle for less sophisticated systems which can be built using simpler techniques and fourth-generation languages.

REFERENCES

1. Michael A. Jackson, *System Development*, Prentice-Hall International, London, 1983.
2. Michael A. Jackson, *Principles of Program Design*, Academic Press Inc. (London) Ltd., London, 1975.

Higher-Order
Software

8.1 WHAT IS HIGHER-ORDER SOFTWARE?

Higher-order software (HOS) is software developed by two brilliant mathematicians, Margaret Hamilton and Saydean Zeldin, for the Apollo space program. It is the first software which is mathematically proven to be correct and this correctness can be verified at every stage of the design process. HOS is sold by Higher-Order Software, Inc. (HOS), of Cambridge, Massachusetts. It can be used by analysts after a two-day course. The most remarkable part of the software and the methodology is that the complex mathematics behind the software need not be understood to be applied.

This chapter is based on the book *Program Design Which Is Provably Correct* by James Martin [1] and on the article "Bug-Free Systems" by Pieter Mimno [2]. HOS is a brilliant step forward into the future of computing. The world of systems analysts and designers must thank James Martin for spelling out in very simple language the principles used in HOS. By so doing, he has brought HOS to the attention of the systems community in a manner that the nonmathematician can understand and relate to.

Before the reader gets carried away by the effectiveness and power of HOS, it is worth emphasizing that the principles on which HOS is based cannot be applied effectively without the software. The strength of HOS lies in the "once only" development of primitive operations which are mathematically correct and the building-block approach to use these primitives through a library or dictionary. To attempt to achieve this manually, even with an understanding of the mathematics, would be a colossal and impractical task. This chapter is intended to provide the reader with enough insight on HOS so that he can decide whether to pursue the subject.

8.2 TESTING AND DEBUGGING SYSTEMS

Every module, program, subsystem, and system must be tested before it is installed. The primary purpose of this testing is to identify problems with the product and only secondarily to determine whether it will work. Martin describes testing as being similar to searching for flying saucers and stating there are none just because you do not find any. If the design were mathematically correct, the amount of testing for errors that could be required would be considerably reduced and would be directed at the outputs and not at the process logic.

Testing can be categorized as "black box" or output testing, and as "white box" or logic testing. What HOS reduces is the amount of white-box testing, as the software proves the logic to be mathematically correct. HOS does not guarantee that the user's requirements have been met because this depends on how effectively they were specified. But HOS can assist in the specification, as it can be used to define the user's needs beginning from the highest levels once they are known. The determination of these needs can be done using the system design techniques described earlier.

8.3 HOS BINARY TREES

HOS is based on binary tree structures. Figure 8.1 illustrates both binary trees and networks which are not trees. The simplest form of binary tree has one parent and two children. Each child, in turn, has two more or no children. No child can have more than one parent. Each tree can be divided into subtrees and each subtree is also a binary tree structure.

Each parent or child is called a *node*. The parent of the tree is called the *root* and the children with no children of their own are called *leaves*. (The terminology is similar to that used in data-base design.) Figure 8.2 illustrates the node as a function that has both input and output. Each function is described as a mathematical equation:

$$y = f(x)$$

where y is the output, f is the function, and x represents the input variables applied to the function.

Binary trees are called *control maps*. Each of the leaf nodes in a control map can be one of four types: P, a primitive operation; OP, an operation defined elsewhere; R, a recursive operation; and XO, an external operation.

P: A *primitive operation* is one that cannot be broken down further.

OP: An *operation defined elsewhere* is one where the operation is expanded in another location.

R: A *recursive operation* is a loop or recursion executed during iteration in a program or module.

XO: An *external operation* is an operation developed outside HOS. An example could be a supplier's software which interfaces with an HOS system. Needless to say, HOS cannot vouch for the correctness of external procedures.

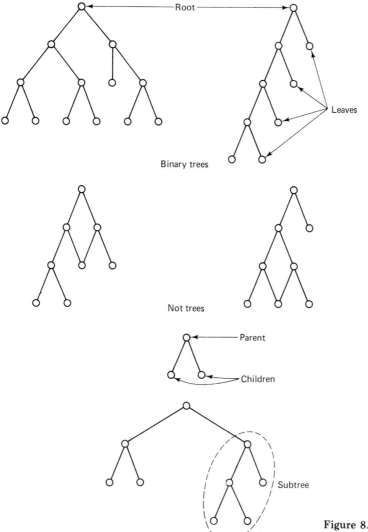

Figure 8.1 Examples of tree structures.

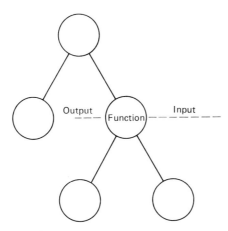

Figure 8.2 Binary tree showing input, output, and function.

8.4 HOS CONTROL STRUCTURES

The three basic logical constructs used in structured English and in programming are sequence, iteration, and selection. Similarly, HOS uses three basic or primitive constructs called *Join*, *Include*, and *Or*. It also uses four extensions of these primitives, referred to as *co-controls*, called *CoJoin*, *CoInclude*, *CoOr*, and *Concur*. We will look at these constructs and at the HOS hierarchy using a very simple example of a bicycle assembly.

8.4.1 Primitives

For simplicity, let us assume that the basic components used to assemble a bicycle are steel tubing for the frame and steel wire for the spokes. Ignore the multitude of other parts that are required. In Figure 8.3, the first operation tells us that a bicycle is assembled using steel wire and steel tubing.

8.4.1.1 Join. We could expand the assembly into two operations, Make Parts and Assemble Parts. We get the wheels and the frame from the Make Parts and these are input to the Assemble Parts. The wheels and frame are not output from the system and hence are internal variables. When the output from the right-hand operation is the input to the left-hand operation, we have a Join executed. In a Join, the input to the right-hand operation has the same input as the parent.

8.4.1.2 Include. The frame and the wheels are manufactured separately and we have two operations, Make Frame using steel tubing and Make Wheels using steel wire. When two independent operations are combined, we have an Include executed. Here the children's inputs are combined to form the parent's.

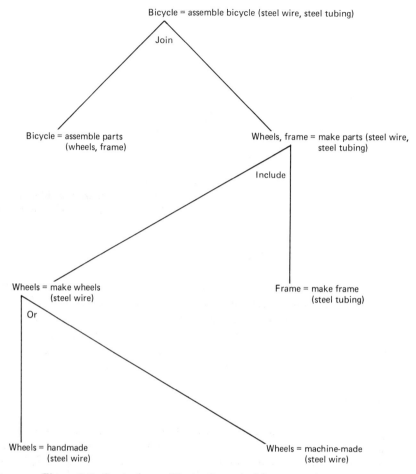

Figure 8.3 Control map illustrating primitive control structures.

8.4.1.3 Or.   The wheels could be machine made or hand made. In both instances, the input is the same steel wire. Where the inputs of the children in the selection are common and are common to the input to the parent, we have an Or executed.

8.4.2 Co-controls

The primitive control structures are very confining and the HOS methodology has been expanded to include more comprehensive controls, each of which has been developed from the primitives.

8.4.2.1 Concur.   In Figure 8.4, the first operation tells us that a bicycle has a manufacturer who builds bicycles whose input consists of capital, location, nuts, bolts, and so on. The manufacturer requires capital and a location. This manufacturer assembles the bicycles using nuts, bolts, steel wire, and so on. In Concur, the output from the right-hand child operation is input to the left-hand operation and is output from the parent. Concur has features from Join and Include.

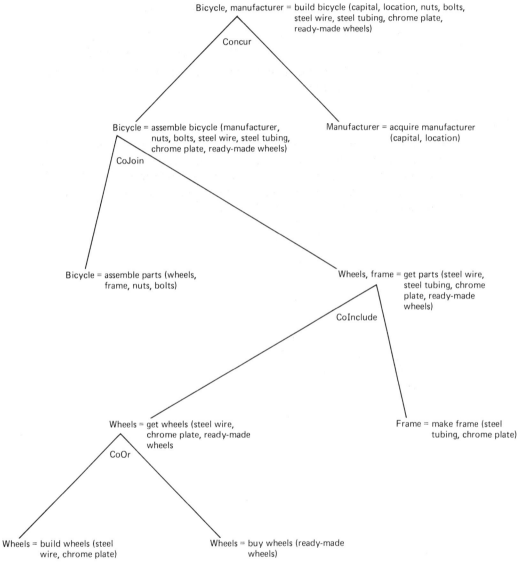

Figure 8.4 Control map illustrating co-control structures.

8.4.2.2 CoJoin.   To assemble the bicycle, we need parts in addition to steel wire and steel tubing. We add nuts, bolts, chrome plate, and ready-made wheels. We get steel wire, steel tubing, chrome plate, and ready-made wheels to build the wheels and frame. The wheels and frame are used to assemble the bicycles using nuts and bolts. In CoJoin, an input to the parent need not be input to the children: for example, the manufacturer. Further, the left-hand child operation could have inputs other than those output from the right-hand operation: for example, the nuts and bolts.

8.4.2.3 CoInclude.   The wheels and frame are obtained separately. In Co-Include, they share common inputs: for example, the chrome plate.

8.4.2.4 CoOr.   The wheels may be bought or built. In CoOr, the inputs to the children are different.

8.5 *N*-ARY BRANCHES

HOS uses a diagramming shorthand which eliminates intermediary parent operations and results in what appears to be a parent with multiple children. The two diagrams shown in Figure 8.5 express the same logic. The difference between them is the elimination of operations I1 and I2 in part (a). We will use this shorthand in our case-study example.

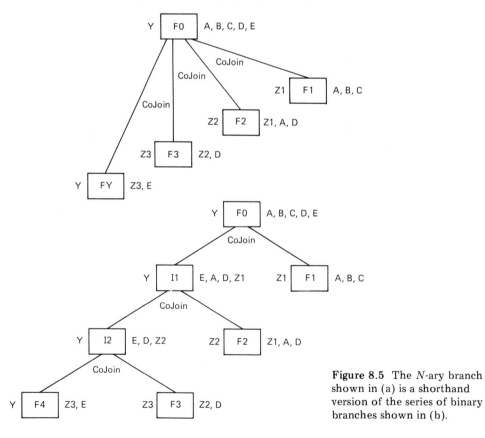

Figure 8.5 The *N*-ary branch shown in (a) is a shorthand version of the series of binary branches shown in (b).

8.6 LOOPS AND RECURSIONS

Iterations in program logic are expressed as "do . . . while . . ." or "repeat . . . until . . ." loops or recursions. Figure 8.6 illustrates how these loops can be handled in HOS. We will see how this type of loop is handled in real life in our case-study example.

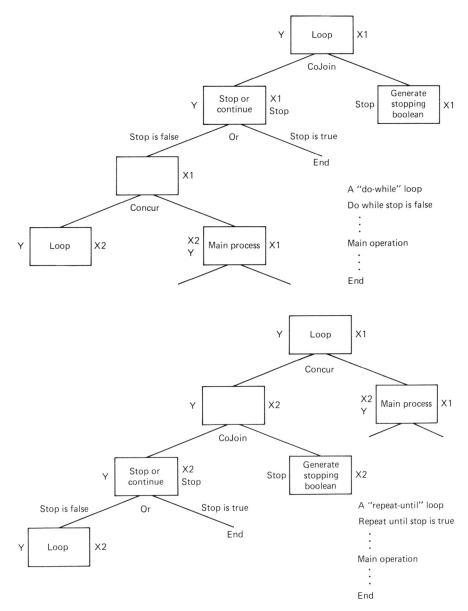

Figure 8.6 Loops.

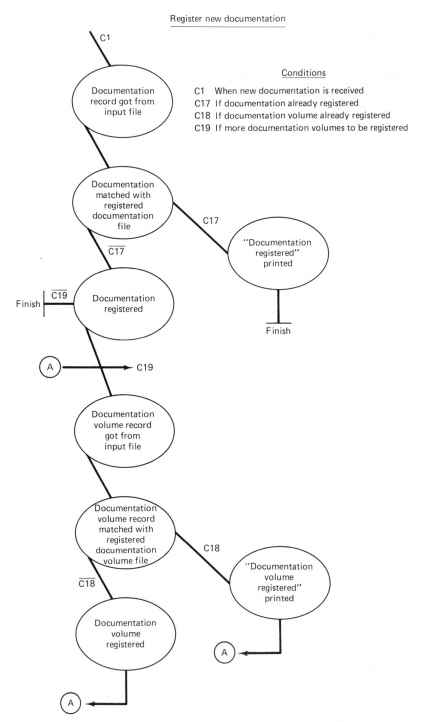

Figure 8.7 Register new documentation procedure from Figure 4.13.

8.7 THE LIBRARY SYSTEM

In Chapter 4 we developed a procedure for registering new documentation received in the library. This procedure is shown in Figure 4.13 and is reproduced with some minor modifications in Figure 8.7. In the original version, the input was keyed on-line. Here we assume that the input is stored and is part of a batch process.

In this procedure, we register the Documentation record and the Documentation Volume records associated with the Documentation. These two events, although linked together, are independent. Figure 8.8 is a control map showing the Register Documentation Record and Process Documentation Volume Record linked by an Include.

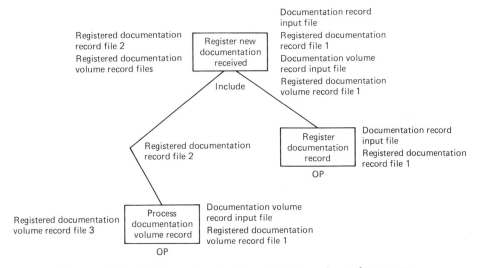

Figure 8.8 Control map showing the registration of new documentation process from Figure 4.13.

Figure 8.9 expands Register Documentation Record. The leaf nodes match the events in Figure 8.7 which relate to Documentation Registration. The reader should note the use of the *n*-ary shorthand in this control map.

We know that there can be several Documentation Volumes. In Figure 8.7, this looping or recursion is indicated by Condition C19. This is illustrated using HOS in Figure 8.10. Figure 8.11 is identical to Figure 8.9, except that Documentation record is replaced by Documentation Volume record. The leaves match the events in Figure 8.7, which relate to the Documentation Volume Registration. The reader should study Figures 8.8 to 8.11 and compare them with Figure 8.7 to gain an appreciation of how HOS is applied to a real-life procedure.

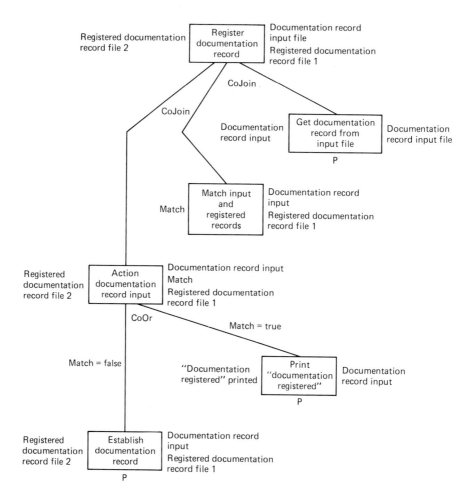

Figure 8.9 Control map for register documentation volume record.

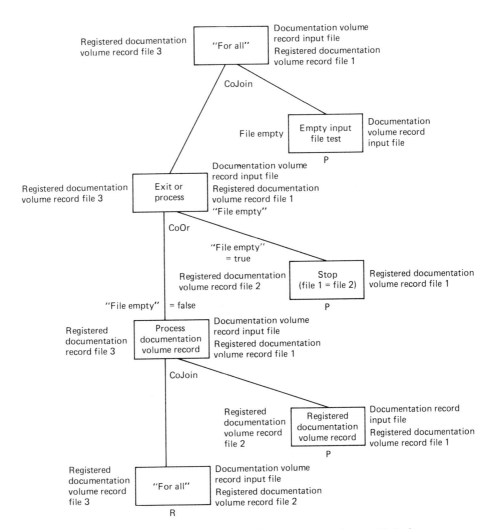

Figure 8.10 Control map showing a loop for processing multiple documentation volume records input.

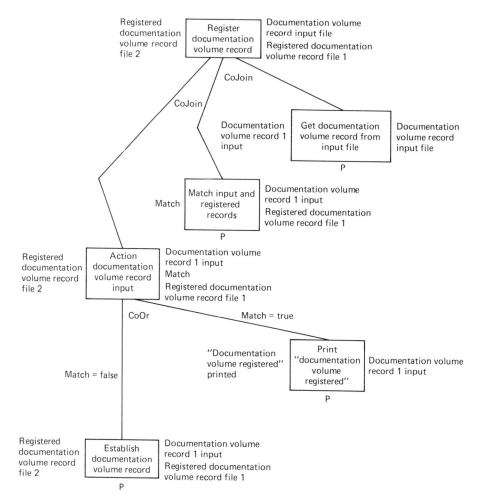

Figure 8.11 Control map for register documentation volume record.

8.8 USE.IT SOFTWARE

USE.IT software [3] is used to execute the HOS methodology. USE.IT has three major components, called AXES, ANALYZER, and RAT. These are shown in Figure 8.12.

AXES is the language used for describing the functions, data types, and control structures. The hierarchies described in this chapter are input to AXES. AXES can accept functions, inputs, and outputs at any level in a system hierarchy. AXES has an interactive component and a textual component which also provides the input to ANALYZER.

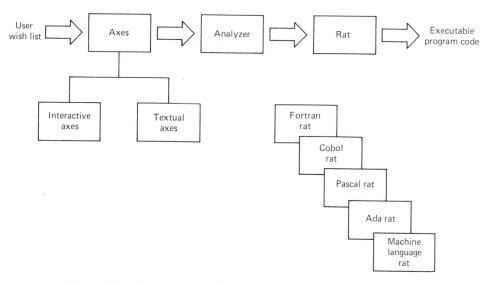

Figure 8.12 Components of USE.IT, the software for implementing the HOS methodology.

ANALYZER checks that the mathematical rules have been obeyed. It also checks for syntactical errors, correct data type transfers, omissions, or inconsistencies in the data types and function descriptions.

RAT (Resource Allocation Tool) uses the output from ANALYZER and generates executable program code. Several versions of RAT are available, including FORTRAN, COBOL, Pascal, and Ada.

8.9 USE.IT ANALYTICAL PROCESS

The USE.IT analytical process is shown in Figure 8.13. The systems analyst, working with the user, creates the system specifications. These specifications can be produced using any of the techniques described in this book. The analyst converts these specifications to control maps and enters these control maps into AXES through the interactive graphics editor. This information is fed to ANALYZER, which checks its correctness and feeds back errors that are found. RAT then produces the executable program code, which can be "black box" (output)-tested.

The USE.IT analytical process is carried out by the analyst and the user. The only programming support required is to interface with external programs produced outside the HOS methodology. This capability, aided by a built-up in-house HOS program library, makes HOS effective as a fourth-generation language and also ensures the mathematical correctness of the program code.

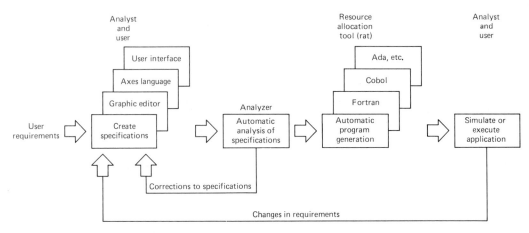

Figure 8.13 Overview of the USE.IT application process.

8.10 ADVANTAGES AND DISADVANTAGES OF HOS

Advantages

1. The strongest feature of HOS is the mathematical correctness of the program code. For example, an internal variable cannot be lost. Further, any change made to the system is input and checked by ANALYZER and its impact is identified before the program is changed. This eliminates the type of horror story one encounters because a minor change made to a system or to a file sets up a chain reaction somewhere else.

2. Procedural languages, such as COBOL or PL/1, require competent and effective programmers to produce correct code. HOS produces this code without programmer participation.

3. System testing at all levels is reduced to "black box" or output testing only. This reduces the time and cost of the testing.

Disadvantages

1. HOS requires a front-end system specification before it can be used. It is not a system design technique similar to the techniques discussed in this book.

REFERENCES

1. James Martin, *Program Design Which Is Provably Correct*, Savant Research Studies, 2 New Street, Carnforth, Lancashire, LA5 9BX, England, 1982.

2. Pieter Mimno, "Bug-Free Systems," *Computerworld*, October 11, 1982.

3. *USE.IT Reference Manual*, Higher-Order Software, Inc., Cambridge, Massachusetts.

9

System
Prototyping

9.1 WHAT IS A PROTOTYPE?

A *prototype* is defined in *Webster's New Collegiate Dictionary* as (1) "an original or model on which something is patterned" and (2) "a first full-scale and usually functional form of a new type or design of a construction (as an airplane)." In system design, prototyping can satisfy either definition. In some instances, the prototype is only a model for further development; in other situations, it can be the full-scale functional system.

The concept of prototyping came into being because software tools became available which made the building of system prototypes a relatively simple exercise. These software tools can be grouped under two broad headings: fourth-generation languages and application generators.

A *fourth-generation language* is a nonprocedural language such as FOCUS or RAMIS in which the code tells the system what to do, not how to do it. (A procedural language such as COBOL uses instructions that define how the procedure should function.)

An *application generator* runs on-line under software such as IBM's CICS/VS transaction processing monitor and eliminates or reduces the programming of system functions such as adding to, updating, or deleting data from a file, and browsing through or inquiring from a file. Some have added features such as screen map and transaction generation, automatic data dictionary update, and file definition. Examples of application generators are IBM's DMS/CICS/VS and Cincom's MANTIS.

A point to be borne in mind is the cost of future maintenance. If the system is built using prototyping software, the cost of maintenance should be a fraction of the cost of using a procedural language such as COBOL.

9.2 WHAT HAPPENS WHEN YOU PROTOTYPE?

The term "prototyping a system" is becoming more common and appears to convey the impression that a user by himself or in cooperation with a systems analyst can build a prototype system easily and in much less time than it takes to build a conventional system. There is some truth in this, but it can be misconstrued and the resulting costs in time and effort can be much higher than the benefits obtained.

We know that the components of a system are the input data, the output data, the file structures, and the system logic to maintain the files and produce the outputs. Other factors that influence the design are its efficiency (which is a measure of its processing speed, core usage, and file organization), the controls, and the data security that may be required.

If we assume that efficiency, controls, and data security can be ignored in the prototype, we are left with the input data, the output data, the file structures, and the system logic. The ideal prototyping software would then generate the input and output screens, the internal files (files under the control of the prototyping software) and the data dictionary, the transactions to update the internal and external files (including data-base management systems), and would produce the outputs. Different fourth-generation languages and application generators may possess some or all of these features, which are shown graphically in Figure 9.1. Let us assume that we have available a software product that will do all these things.

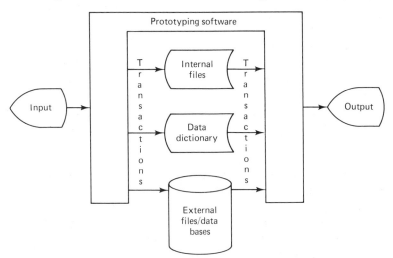

Figure 9.1 Flow of data through ideal prototyping software to develop a system.

What the user or the user and the analyst then have to do is to design the file structures, including the records and the data elements, the input screens, and the output screens, and provide transaction logic other than add, delete, and update functions, which the software will provide. Let us assume also that all this is done directly on-line with the software prompting the design.

9.3 CAN A SYSTEM BE PROTOTYPED WITHOUT A SPECIFICATION?

The impression that one is left with at this point is that with this powerful tool, any system that the user requires can be modeled without any additional information being provided. As the user is interested primarily in his outputs, he designs all the possible screens that he may require to meet his needs. The software accepts the screen designs and produces the screen maps so that these screens can now be called when specific outputs are required.

Now comes the crunch! How are these output data to be organized in the internal and external files or data bases? Is it sufficient to identify each output record as a record in file? What are the possibilities of data redundancy in different records in the same file? Worse, what about data redundancy, inconsistency, and incompatibility between different files accessed by the system? Will the data dictionary solve all these problems? When and how is the file update and output production logic defined?

The reader will probably recognize these issues, as they have all been covered in the various system design techniques described in the text. The answer, then, to the question "Can a system be prototyped without a specification?" is a very definite "no!" What should be done is to combine the use of prototyping software with good system design techniques. This combination can result in the fast, effective development of systems which really meet the user's needs. On the other hand, not all the techniques lend themselves to prototyping.

9.4 PROTOTYPING AND THE SYSTEM DESIGN TECHNIQUES

9.4.1 Information Engineering

The principal outputs from information engineering are a normalized logical data structure, procedures for maintaining the records in the data structure, and procedures for producing the output records and screens. These solve the problems we encountered when we attempted to design the file structures using the prototyping software. So, we can expect information engineering and prototyping software to blend together successfully.

9.4.2 Structured Analysis and Design

The outputs from structured analysis and design are data flow diagrams, minispecifications, normalized file structures, structure charts, program specifications, and a data dictionary. The emphasis here is on the specification of a logical data flow diagram of the user's requirements which is converted to a physical data flow diagram which, in turn, becomes the basis for the system design using the structure chart as a design tool.

It is difficult to justify how prototyping software can be used usefully in conjunction with these features other than as a programming aid after the structured design process is complete. It could be argued that the data flows defined in the final physical data flow diagram could provide the output and input definitions. Further, we also have a normalized data structure. What is to prevent us from prototyping? Nothing. But if we do prototype, we are no longer using structured design and in particular the structure chart. Instead, we are using the prototyping software to produce our file maintenance and output programs.

It could be argued again that what has been developed is only a "model" —that the "real" system will be designed using structured design and structure charts. This could be done but would be a case of writing the specifications after obtaining a working system. The designers could then use a procedural language such as COBOL to code the system. This may be justified in terms of system efficiency. Before rewriting the entire system in COBOL or PL/1, it would be worthwhile converting and testing one subsystem or one large program to see if there are any real savings to be obtained in processing time or core usage.

9.4.3 Structured Requirements Definition

The principal outputs from structured requirements definition are the mainline functional flow diagrams and the application results. These provide the output and input definitions and the transactions needed to prototype. What is missing is the file structure. In Chapter 6, we identified this as a problem. If this is overcome, prototyping software can be used in conjunction with structured requirements definition, but only after mainline functional flow diagrams, the file definition, and the application results (outputs) are defined.

9.4.4 Jackson System Development

JSD consists of six steps, and only in the sixth step is the concept of a "file" introduced. Before this step, it is assumed that every entity exists by itself and is processed on its own independent processor. Also, during the five preceding steps, the process has been defined in considerable detail in procedural language assuming that coding will be done using a language such as COBOL or PL/1. Prototyping software could be used after Step 6. But if it is used, the cost and effort of developing the detailed specifications in Steps 1 to 5 could be wasted. Further, the time-oriented systems that are suited to JSD may not lend themselves to prototyping.

9.5 PROTOTYPING PHYSICAL FILES AND DATA BASES

The subject of prototyping physical files and data bases is mentioned here only because this activity is often confused with system prototyping. This misunderstanding occurs because in both situations we are dealing with physical files.

The objective of system prototyping is to obtain either a working model of the proposed system which can be built using the model as a specification with procedural languages such as COBOL, or a model which can be expanded to become the proposed system. In system prototyping, we design a logical file structure which we convert into a physical file either using the prototyping software or a file or data base that is accessed by the prototyping software. The emphasis, in this activity, is to define the physical file structure in terms of records and record relationships or associations, map the input and output screens, and define and develop the transactions for file maintenance and output production. The result is a working system.

The objective of physical file or data-base prototyping is to obtain the most efficient file or data-base organization for the production file or data base. This is done by simulating the production file in terms of record volumes, file accesses, and access paths through the file or data base. The tool used is special software which simulates these features in the file or data base. Undoubtedly, if a working prototype system is available, this simulation becomes much simpler, as the prototype system eliminates the need for programs or modules to be produced to add, delete, modify, read, or extract data from the simulated file.

Application System Development Methodologies

During the 1970s it was recognized that large and complex systems were being built with virtually no management control, resulting in high-cost overruns and late delivery of the systems, if they were delivered at all. Further, systems that were delivered often did not meet the users' requirements and were supported by poor or nonexistent documentation, which made system maintenance and enhancement a nightmare.

Nature abhors a vacuum, and two types of solutions appeared. The first was the design and development of a variety of system design techniques such as the techniques discussed in this text. The second was the advent of application systems development methodologies (ASDMs). The latter were project management tools that divided the entire specification, design, development, and implementation process into a series of phases, activities, and tasks. Each phase, activity, and task had standard outputs (deliverables) defined, and at specific checkpoints, user management could decide whether or not to proceed. These methodologies or project control systems were developed by the organizations that used them and by vendors.

Management found that now they had control over system development and insisted that these "standards" be adhered to. This meant that any system being planned, developed, and implemented had to follow the "standard" project plan and produce the "standard" outputs or deliverables. This proved to be both a blessing and a curse.

It was a blessing because the standards gave management tight control over the total process. The auditors and the quality control staff loved it because at last they could demand specific documentation in specific formats containing specific information. It was a curse because the standard specifications were either in narrative form and too general to convert into a system design which effectively met the user's requirements, or too specific and directed at particular design techniques, ruling out the use of other techniques.

There is no general solution to this problem, as the problem itself is different in every organization. So the reader and his organization have to solve their own problem themselves. To give the reader an appreciation of the type of situation that he could encounter, we describe here the type of information required and a generalized model of an application system development methodology. We then superimpose the various design techniques on the model and discuss their impact.

10.1 OUTPUTS FROM SYSTEM DEVELOPMENT

The outputs or deliverables from system development can be classified under four basic headings:

1. Management decision-making information
2. Project management information
3. System design and maintenance information
4. System operating information

10.1.1 Management Decision-Making Information

Management decision-making information is the information management needs to make "go"/"no go" types of decisions. These include costs and benefits, delivery dates, organizational impacts, and impacts on other systems.

10.1.2 Project Management Information

Project management information is the information the project manager needs to plan and control the project. It includes planned and achieved schedules, planned and achieved costs, and products delivered. Tools used to manage the project include critical path diagrams and project control software.

10.1.3 System Development and Maintenance Information

System development and maintenance information is the information used in the specification, design, construction, and implementation of the system which is needed to maintain and enhance the system after it is implemented. The foregoing chapters have described the type of information to be produced.

10.1.4 System Operating Information

System operating information is the information needed to run the system after it is implemented. In a batch system, this could include computer operator instructions, input and output handling information, and delivery schedules. In an on-line system, this could include network information, terminal operator instructions, and transaction processing monitor (such as IBM's CICS/VS) information. In both, the user's manual procedures would always be included.

10.1.5 Problems with Standard Outputs

In general, problems encountered in defining the management decision-making information, the project control information, and the operating information are a function of management policy and the computer operating environment in a particular organization. But problems encountered with system specification and design information are a function of the system specification and design techniques used. The latter is hard to understand, as the argument that is put forward is that the requirement is for a set of design "blueprints" and accompanying documentation. If this works for airplanes, bridges, and houses, why does it not work for computer systems?

In the cases of airplanes, houses, and bridges, the blueprints reflect "what" is to be delivered. In computer systems specification and design, the design documents reflect primarily "how" the system has been designed. So the possibilities for differences in specification and design approaches are endless. The next question that can be asked is: Why "how" and not "what"? The answer is that a part of the design and maintenance information is "what" information. This encompasses logical and physical file structures, record and data definitions, program code, system and subsystem content, and input and output definitions. The "how" information describes how the "what" information was obtained.

Computer systems are a constantly changing entity, unlike airplanes, bridges, and houses. To keep up with this constant change, the staff that maintain and enhance these systems must have access to the "how" information to save them time and effort that could be wasted "reinventing the wheel." That is why the "how" information is so critical.

10.2 GENERALIZED MODEL OF AN ASDM

The major activities that make up an application system development methodology are as follows:

- Feasibility study
- Business specification
- System specification
- System design
- System development and testing
- System implementation
- System review

10.2.1 Feasibility Study

The *feasibility study* is done to provide management with sufficient information to decide whether to build the system or to take other action. The report that is produced defines the project scope, the user's system's objectives, performance requirements, interfacing systems, a general description of the system to be developed and the alternative choices, the impact on the organization, the impact on the computer environment, the cost of development, the cost of operating the system, the benefits to be obtained, and the risks of not developing the system. It also includes a project plan and a budget and schedule in detail for the next phase or major activity, and an estimated schedule and budget for the total project.

When evaluating the system choices available, the feasibility study must take into account the design techniques that will be used. The information obtained during the feasibility study becomes the foundation for the detailed design to be done later.

10.2.2 Business Specification

The *business specification* is a detailed definition of the user's business needs that should be met by the proposed system. This specification could include the user's operational objectives, a description of the outputs required to meet these objectives and when they are required, the flow of information between organizational entities, the logical processes required to convert input data into file data and file data into output data, and a description of the logical files.

Every author has a different definition of the business specification because his definition fits the particular specification and design technique he advocates. For example, DeMarco's business specification is based on a logical data flow diagram, and Orr's is based on an assembly line diagram and a description of the outputs. At this point the reader is entitled to become confused. Let us examine logically the content of the business specification exclusive of the specification and design techniques.

The user needs information to carry out his functions to meet his objectives. So the most important items to be defined are the objectives and the data needed to meet these objectives. Some organizations might have difficulty defining objectives but could probably define their functions. If we assume that these functions involve processes to meet objectives (even if undefined), we can define the data needed to carry out these functions.

Having defined the data, we need to store them so that we can access them when needed. This means organizing the data into logical groupings. These groupings consist of allied items of data or records. As we will be dealing with many such records, we need to define logical record files. These data must be obtained from somewhere. So we need to define the data sources or the inputs. Similarly, the data must be formatted before they can be used. So we need to define the outputs. The user may decide that he does not need specific outputs but may choose to access the files to obtain data to meet specific needs as they arise. If this is the case, we do not need to define the outputs. The outputs or the data in the files will be needed by the user at particular times, such as immediately, daily, weekly, and so on. So we need to define the response times for each output. The organization may be centralized or decentralized, requiring either centralized or decentralized files or data bases.

The data input may not be in the format in which it is filed and may need to be logically combined with the file data before being stored. Similarly, the file data may need to be processed to produce data in a different format in the outputs. All this logical data processing needs to be defined as a set of logical procedures.

To sum up, the business specification consists of:

- Definition of the business objectives or the functions
- Definition of the data required to meet the objectives or the functions
- Definition of the logical records and files
- Definition of the data input
- Definition of the outputs (if required)
- Identification of when output or file data are required
- Identification of the need for centralized or decentralized files or data bases
- Definitions of the input process logic
- Definitions of the output process logic (if required)

The business specification, like the feasibility study, includes a detailed budget and schedule for the next phase and an updated estimate of the budget and schedule to the end of the project.

10.2.3 System Specification

The *system specification* is the division of the business specification into computerized and manual processes. It also includes descriptions of how the system could function, for example, on-line update and retrieval, overnight batch update and on-line retrieval, or a centralized data base with distributed data update and retrieval. The impact of each choice on the organization's hardware and software environment is evaluated. Each system choice is costed and tentatively scheduled. The choices are discussed and appropriate recommendations are made to the user. The user decides which choice to implement. This choice is budgeted and scheduled in detail for the following phase and the total project cost and schedule are updated.

10.2.4 System Design

This phase or major activity is probably better termed *system architecture and design*. The term *architecture* is appropriate because the physical file or data base and network architectures are defined now. The subsystem, program, and module hierarchies are established and the program logic defined in detail. Test plans, file conversion, hardware and software acquisition and installation plans, and implementation strategies are prepared. The project budget and schedule are updated in detail until implementation of the production system is completed.

10.2.5 Development and Testing

During this phase or activity, all modules and programs are coded and tested, and physical files or data bases are established and tested with the coded modules and programs at the program, subsystem, and system levels using the (new) hardware and software. Forms and screens are designed, user procedures written, and operational documentation prepared. In short, the system is built and tested by the builders, the designers, and the users.

10.2.6 System Implementation

System implementation involves the training of operating staff and users, conversion of files and data bases, organizational changes (if necessary), the protection of production programs and modules, and the installation of security controls for access to data in the files or data bases.

10.2.7 System Review

During a *system review*, the system is examined to determine whether the user's requirements are being met and to tune the system to improve system processing efficiency.

10.3 THE ASDM AND THE SYSTEM DESIGN TECHNIQUES

We can assume that a feasibility study is necessary, regardless of the design technique to be used, accepting that the design technique will influence the system choices described and costed. We can also assume that the design technique will not play a major role during the development, testing, and implementation of the system because, at this time, the files and data bases have been defined, and the subsystems, programs, and modules have been specified in detail. This leaves three phases or activities that must be matched against each design technique: the business specification, the system specification, and the system design. For the benefit of the reader, the outputs from these activities, excluding project control information, are summarized in Table 10.1.

To determine whether ASDMs are independent of information system specification and design techniques, let us examine the four techniques described in this text and how they interface with the generalized ASDM described above. The four are information engineering (James Martin and Clive Finkelstein), structured analysis and design (Tom DeMarco, Edward Yourdon, and Larry Constantine), structured requirements definition (Ken Orr), and Jackson system development (Michael Jackson). We will also comment on how higher-order software (HOS) and prototyping may be combined with some of the other techniques in an ASDM. In our examination, we will identify only those activities and outputs from the techniques which are relevant to this discussion.

10.3.1 Information Engineering

The information engineering activities we will examine are information analysis, procedure formation, implementation strategies, and program specification synthesis.

In information analysis, the business objectives to be met by the system are defined together with the data required to meet these objectives. The output from information analysis is a normalized data model which can provide all the output data required from the system. If distributed processing was included in the objectives, the data model should reflect either a centralized data structure or a series of distributed data models to meet the

TABLE 10.1 FEASIBILITY, SPECIFICATION, AND DESIGN OUTPUTS
(EXCLUDING PROJECT CONTROL INFORMATION)

Feasibility study

Project scope
User's system objectives
Performance requirements
Interfacing systems
General description of system to be developed with alternate choices
Impact on the organization
Impact on the computer environment
Development cost
Operating cost
Benefits and risks

Business specification

Definition of the business objectives or the functions
Definition of the data required to meet the objectives or the functions
Definition of the logical records and files
Definition of the data input
Definition of the outputs (if required)
Identification of when output or file data are required
Identification of the need for centralized or decentralized files or data bases
Definitions of the input process logic
Definitions of the output process logic (if required)

System specification

Logical system divided into computerized and manual processes
Possible implementation options, such as on-line and batch update, on-line data
access, and so on, with their associated costs, benefits, and estimated development schedules

System design

Physical file or data-base design
Network design
Physical architecture of subsystems and programs
Detailed program and module logic
Test plans
File conversion plans
Hardware and software acquisition and installation plans
Implementation strategies

distributed file or data-base needs. In procedure formation, the logical input
and output processes are defined together with the inputs and outputs. The
output information should include when the outputs are required. Hence
the business specification can be obtained using information engineering
(Table 10.2).

In system specification, we divide the system into computerized and
manual processes. We also discuss possible implementation options, such as
on-line and batch update, on-line data access, and so on, with their asso-

TABLE 10.2 INFORMATION ENGINEERING: BUSINESS SPECIFICATION

	Information analysis	Procedure formation	Implementation strategies	Program specification synthesis
Business objectives and/or functions	Yes			
Data required by the objectives or the functions	Normalized data model			
Logical records/file definition	Yes			
Data input		Yes		
Output (if required)		Yes		
When output or file data required		Yes		
Centralized/decentralized files or data bases	Yes			
Input process logic		Event diagram condition tables, LAMs, and DADs		
Output process logic (if required)		Yes		

TABLE 10.3 INFORMATION ENGINEERING: SYSTEM SPECIFICATION

	Information analysis	Procedure formation	Imple- mentation strategies	Program specification synthesis
Logical system into computerized and manual processes			Yes	
Implementation options			Yes	

ciated costs, benefits, and estimated development schedules. In information engineering, these activities are the front end to the activity termed *implementation strategies* (Table 10.3).

The system design activity or phase includes physical file or data-base design, network design, the physical architecture of the subsystems and programs, and detailed program and module logic. In information engineering, the file, data base, and network design is covered under physical data-base design. The subsystem and program architecture, and the detailed program and module logic, are part of program specification synthesis. Test plans, file conversion plans, hardware and software acquisition, and installation plans are part of the activity termed *implementation strategies* (Table 10.4).

TABLE 10.4 INFORMATION ENGINEERING: SYSTEM DESIGN

	Information analysis	Procedure formation	Imple- mentation strategies	Program specification synthesis
Physical file or data-base design	This is a specific activity in information engineering.			
Network design			Yes	
Physical architecture of subsystems/ programs			Yes	
Detailed program and module logic				Yes
Test plans			Yes	
File conversion plans			Yes	
Hardware and software acquisition and installation plans			Yes	
Implementation strategies			Yes	

We can conclude that information engineering can be superimposed on the business specification, system specification, and the system design activities in the ASDM. But when it is superimposed, the information engineering and ASDM activities overlap. Although the ASDM's outputs can be produced, a project control plan established for the ASDM will not fit information engineering unless the information engineering activities are subdivided and reorganized under the ASDM.

10.3.2 Structured Analysis and Design

The structured analysis and design activities are grouped under three main headings: structured analysis, structured design, and implementation.

In structured analysis, although the business objectives are not defined, the system functions provide the basis for the proposed logical data flow diagram, the minispecifications, and the data dictionary. The data dictionary contains information on the inputs and the outputs from the system. The minispecifications define the process logic. In addition, a normalized logical data structure is produced. Although not mentioned in DeMarco's text (*Structured Analysis and System Specification*), it can be assumed that distributed processing could affect the logical file structures and the data flow diagrams. Identification of when the outputs are required is left until the structured design activity. Hence the new logical environment defines the business specification excluding the "response" times required (Table 10.5).

TABLE 10.5 STRUCTURED ANALYSIS AND DESIGN: BUSINESS SPECIFICATION

	Structured analysis	Structured design	Implementation
Business objectives and/or functions	Yes		
Data required by the objectives or the functions	Data dictionary		
Logical records/file definition	Normalized data structure		
Data input	Data dictionary		
Output (if required)	Data dictionary		
When output or file data required		Yes	
Centralized/decentralized files or data bases	Yes		
Input process logic	Proposed logical DFD and minispecs		
Output process logic (if required)	Proposed logical DFD and minispecs		

The structured specification includes the partition of the proposed logical data flow diagram into computerized and manual processes, and the identification of the different physical options available with estimated costs, benefits, and schedules. This is the output required from system specification (Table 10.6).

TABLE 10.6 STRUCTURED ANALYSIS AND DESIGN: SYSTEM SPECIFICATION

	Structured analysis	Structured design	Implementation
Logical system into computerized and manual processes	Yes		
Implementation options	Yes		

The outputs from structured design are the structure charts packaged into physical modules and programs, and the detailed program and module logic. Not mentioned in Yourdon and Constantine's *Structured Design*, but implied, is the physical design of the files or data bases and the networks. Also not specifically mentioned but assumed are the test plans, file conversion plans, hardware and software acquisition and installation plans, and the implementation strategies (Table 10.7).

TABLE 10.7 STRUCTURED ANALYSIS AND DESIGN: SYSTEM DESIGN

	Structured analysis	Structured design	Implementation
Physical file or data-base design			Yes
Network design			Yes
Physical architecture of subsystems/programs		Structure chart	
Detailed program and module logic		Yes	
Test plans			Yes
File conversion plans			Yes
Hardware and software acquisition and installation plans			Yes
Implementation strategies			Yes

With minor variations, structured analysis and design closely complement the ASDM process and provide the required ASDM outputs. A generalized project control plan developed for the ASDM could be expanded to fit structured analysis and design as described by DeMarco, Yourdon, and Constantine.

10.3.3 Structured Requirements Definition

Structured requirements definition consists of two major classes of activities: logical definition and physical definition. Logical definition is subdivided into the application context definition, the application functions, and the application results.

The mainline functional flow diagram, which is an assembly line diagram for the system, together with the process descriptions and the application results or outputs, describes the logical system. This logical system is based on the system functions and the flow of data between organizational entities. "When the output data are provided" is implicit in mainline functional flow diagrams. The logical records and files are organized into logical structures, but Orr's text (*Structured Requirements Definition*) does not indicate how this is done. No specific mention is made of distributed processing needs, but it can be assumed that they could affect the mainline functional flow and the logical data structures. In general, completion of the logical definition phase provides the outputs for the business specification (Table 10.8).

TABLE 10.8 STRUCTURED REQUIREMENTS DEFINITION: BUSINESS SPECIFICATION

	Logical definition			
	Application context definition	Application functions	Application results	Physical definition
Business objectives and/or functions	Entity diagram and objectives			
Data required by the objectives or the functions			Logical data output: form, content, and structure	
Logical records/file definition			Logical bases files	
Data input			Principal outputs which include inputs	
Output (if required)				
When output or file data required			Organizational cycles	
Centralized/ decentralized files or data bases			Yes	
Input process logic		Assembly line diagrams and mainline functional flow		
Output process logic (if required)				

In the physical definition phase, alternative physical solutions are examined based on computerizing part or all of the logical system. This is in line with the output required from system specification (Table 10.9).

TABLE 10.9 STRUCTURED REQUIREMENTS DEFINITION: SYSTEM SPECIFICATION

	Logical definition			
	Application context definition	Application functions	Application results	Physical definition
Logical system into computerized and manual processes		Expansion of functional flow		
Implementation options				Alternative physical solutions

The system design or the physical design of the system is not discussed in "structured requirements definition," but it is assumed that the physical solution is expanded in sufficient detail to provide the outputs for this activity (Table 10.10).

TABLE 10.10 STRUCTURED REQUIREMENTS DEFINITION: SYSTEM DESIGN

	Logical definition			
	Application context definition	Application functions	Application results	Physical definition
Physical file or data-base design				Yes
Network design				Yes
Physical architecture of subsystems/ programs				Yes
Detailed program and module logic				Yes
Test plans				Yes
File conversion plans				Yes
Hardware and software acquisition and installation plans				Yes
Implementation strategies				Yes

Structured requirements definition, like structured analysis and design, closely complements the ASDM with minor variations. So, a project plan designed for the ASDM can be expanded to cover structured requirements definition.

10.3.4 Jackson System Development

Jackson system development consists of six steps:

1. Entity action
2. Entity structure
3. Initial model
4. Function
5. System timing
6. Implementation

Jackson approaches system development in a unique manner where he identifies entities in Step 1; maps the actions that can be taken on the entities in the real world in Step 2; converts these actions and entities into initial models for computerization in Step 3; adds functions to these models to produce required outputs in Step 4; adds the response or timing requirement to the model in Step 5; and builds and implements the system in Step 6. Further, until Step 5, the design is based on a single processor for each entity.

This approach is completely different from the activities and the outputs described in the ASDM. Readers intending to use JSD should be prepared to develop on their own or acquire from Jackson a project plan or methodology to build JSD systems.

10.3.5 Higher-Order Software

Higher-order software is software which converts a system specification into error-free program code. The conversion of the specification into HOS input is equivalent to system design. Hence any of the design techniques discussed here could provide input to HOS. In some cases the normal system design activity may be replaced completely by the HOS conversion. In other situations, the HOS conversion may complement the system design. Those readers intending to use HOS should analyze their design approach in combination with HOS and arrive at the best combination of activities to satisfy their needs.

10.3.6 Prototyping

Prototyping is not a design technique by itself. Effective prototyping can only be done in conjunction with another system design technique and its use with an ASDM will vary according to the technique with which it is combined.

10.4 STANDARD ASDM OUTPUTS

We stated in Section 10.1.5 that standard outputs could be defined for management decision making, project management, and system operation based on local management policies and the computer operating environment. But system design and maintenance outputs presented problems, as they were heavily influenced by the system specification and design techniques used. The three ASDM activities affected by these problems are the business specification, the system specification, and the system design.

Based on our analysis of the generalized ASDM and the system specification and design techniques, we can conclude that standard outputs can be defined for the business specification, the system specification, and the system design. These generic outputs are listed in Table 10.1. There could always be exceptions to these standards, as we saw with JSD. Further, secondary documentation standards should be defined for the process outputs from each system specification and design technique applied. Examples of such outputs are data flow diagrams, assembly line diagrams, condition tables, event diagrams, LAMs, and DADs. This additional technique-oriented documentation should simplify the tasks of system enhancement and maintenance.

We can conclude further that if an ASDM specifies outputs which are confined to individual techniques such as data flow diagrams or insists on narrative descriptions of specifications, it would probably be rigid and difficult to modify.

Data Use
Analysis

Data use analysis [1] is done to:

- Determine record volumes anticipated to estimate storage requirements.
- Identify logical access paths through the file or data base and their number to highlight the heavily used paths for physical data-base or file design.

A logical file access occurs when a record is accessed in order to be added to, deleted from, modified, or retrieved from a file, or a combination of these events. Accesses can occur on entry to the file or between records. A logical access could be a physical access to a data base or file record, an access to an input/output buffer such as COBOL working storage, or a table in main storage. The information gained from data use analysis will influence the physical data-base or file structure.

There are two ways of identifying the logical access paths through a data model for a particular procedure. The first is to trace the file accesses from the procedure. The second is to use Martin's LAM approach and define the access path before defining the procedure. Here we will follow the first method.

Figure 11.1 is a procedure to "Accept Order and Produce Customer Order." Figure 11.2 defines the contents of Customer Order. Figure 11.3 is a data model called a *transaction usage map* which has the record volumes and the logical accesses drawn on it. The accesses are sequenced and are shown as A, add; M, modify; or R, retrieve. The model also indicates the ratios of records to one another along their association paths.

The first record to be accessed in the model is the Customer record in order to validate the Customer Number input as part of the Order Header

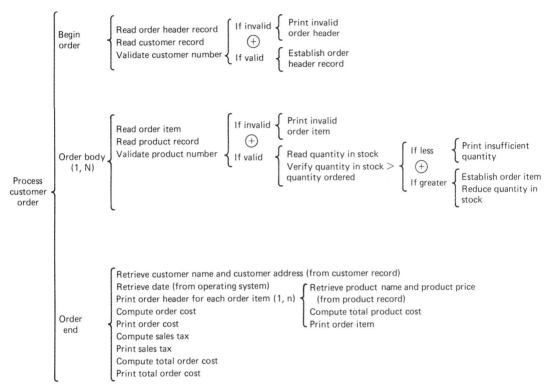

Figure 11.1 "Accept Order and Produce Customer Order" procedure.

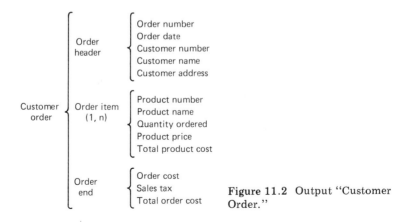

Figure 11.2 Output "Customer Order."

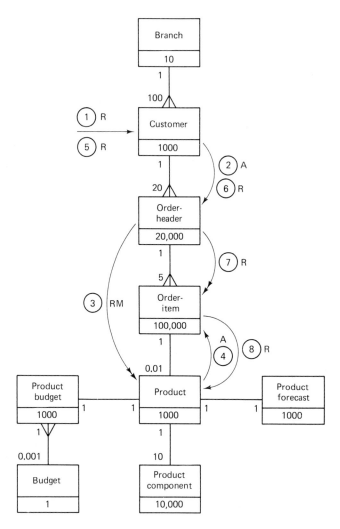

Figure 11.3 Transaction usage map for the "Accept Order and Produce Customer Order" procedure with storage and logical access data shown.

record. This is a retrieval event. If the Customer Number is valid, the second access occurs to establish the Order Header. This is an add event. The third access, to the Product record, occurs to validate the Product Number in each Order Item record input. This is a retrieval event. If the Product Number is valid, the Quantity in Stock is reduced (i.e., the Product record is modified). Then the fourth access occurs to establish the Order Item record. To print the Customer Order, the Customer record, the Order Header record, the Order Item records, and the Product records are accessed (accesses 5 to 8). These accesses are all retrievals, as they do not change the data in the file.

The information recorded in the transaction usage map is recorded in a reference table (Figure 11.4). This table provides the loading on the data base or file in a given period for the transactions associated with a given pro-

No.	Usage path	Type of access	Record volume relationships	Number of logical references		Comments
				Per transaction	Per period	
1	Entry: customer	R	1	1	100	
2	Customer: order header	A	1	1	100	
3	Order header: product	RM	5	5	500	No. of product accesses =
4	Product: order item	A	1	5	500	no. of order items set up
5	Entry: customer	R	1	1	100	Entry repeated
6	Customer: order header	R	1	1	100	
7	Order header: order item	R	5	5	500	
8	Order item: product	R	1	5	500	
				24	2400	

Figure 11.4 Transaction usage map reference table for the "Accept Order and Produce Customer Order" procedure.

cedure. This period could be an hour, a day, or even a week. Its purpose is to provide a common factor for accumulating all transactions from all procedures that access the particular file or data base to determine the total access load.

The first column in Figure 11.4 is the access sequence. The second column is the logical access or usage path. The third is the type of access. The fourth indicates the volume ratios between associated records. If a direct association does not exist (e.g., Order Header and Product), this is derived. Here, each Order Item accesses one Product record, so the ratio of Order Header to Product is the same as Order Header to Order Item (i.e., 1:5).

The fifth column is the number of references per transaction. We derive this number from the product of the Record Volume Relationship and the

No.	Usage path	Number of logical references per period					Total logical references per period
		Procedure A	Procedure B	Procedure C	Procedure D	Procedure E	
1	Entry: customer	200					200
2	Customer: order header	200					200
3	Order header: product	500	300				800
4	Product: order item	500	300				800
5	Order header: order item	500					500
6	Order item: product	500					500
7	Entry: order header		100				100
8	Order header: customer		100				100
9	Product: product forecast					100	100
10	Product: product budget			100			100
11	Product budget: budget			100			100
12	Product: product component				200		200
13	Entry: product			100	200	100	400
		2400	800	300	400	200	4100

Figure 11.5 Consolidated transaction usage map reference table.

Number of Occurrences of the primary record. For example, in usage path 2, Customer is accessed once per transaction and the Record Volume Relationship is 1. Hence $1 \times 1 = 1$. In usage path 4, Product is accessed five times during one transaction and the Record Volume Relationship between Product and Order Item is 1. Hence $5 \times 1 = 5$. The number of Logical References per Period is the product of the Logical References per Transaction and the Number of Entries into the file during the period. The file is entered 100 times per period for this procedure.

In Figure 11.5, the consolidated transaction map, we consolidate the Logical References per Period by procedure. The final column in this chart

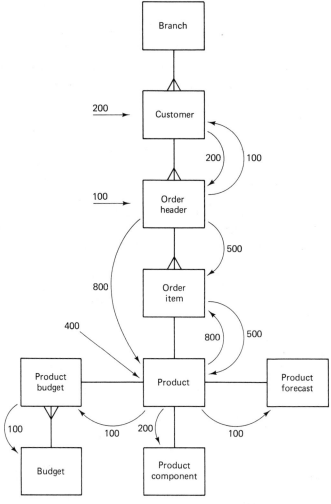

Figure 11.6 Composite load map reflecting the consolidated transactions in Figure 11.5.

gives us the loading by access path and the total accesses to the file during the period. This information is entered on the data model in Figure 11.6 to provide the physical data base or file designer with a graphic view of the logical accesses through the model.

We stated that two objectives should be met by data use analysis. The first was to determine the file storage requirements and the second was to determine the access loading through the file to determine the heavily used paths. Figure 11.3 provides the record volumes and meets objective 1; Figure 11.6 provides the access loading per period and meets objective 2.

REFERENCE

1. James Martin and Clive Finkelstein, *Information Engineering*, Savant Research Studies, 2 New Street, Carnforth, Lancashire LA5 9BX, England, 1981.

12

The Information
Explosion

12.1 CHOOSING THE "RIGHT" SYSTEM DESIGN TECHNIQUE

Six system specification and design techniques or approaches have been discussed in this text. There are probably three times as many available which we have not mentioned. Which of these is the best? Is one really better than another? Can two or more techniques be combined?

I do not personally believe that there is any one best specification and design technique, in the same way as there is no one most beautiful person in the world. Each approach has its good and weak points and only the system designer can say which is best suited to his needs. There may be some merit, though, in combining certain features from different techniques.

12.2 COMBINATIONS OF TECHNIQUES

12.2.1 JSD and Information Engineering

JSD and information engineering, on the surface, appear to have little in common. JSD is a technique for defining and designing dynamic, time-oriented systems. Jackson does not even touch on data bases until Step 6, implementation. Information engineering is a data-base-oriented, static technique. It is static because it is based on snapshots of the static data model which displays associations or relationships between records but does not represent data flow. What they have in common is the entity, which has almost the same meaning in both techniques.

In Steps 1 and 2 of JSD, Jackson defines the entities, the actions performed on the entities, and the structure diagram which models the entities and the actions during the lifetime of the entity. The development of these products gives the user and the analyst a sound understanding of the business and the extent to which the business is to be reflected in the new system. Further, these entities and the action attributes simplify the task of developing the data model in information analysis, and the actions provide an insight into the procedures to be developed in procedure formation.

12.2.2 Information Engineering, Structured Analysis and Design, and Structured Requirements Definition

The common factor between information engineering, structured analysis, and structured requirements definition is the normalized data model. This data model is developed before procedures are identified in information engineering. In structured analysis and structured requirements definition, the model is developed based on the logical files developed from the procedural flow. The latter is acceptable as long as the data in the data model are restricted to the particular system being developed. It is insufficient when organizations are attempting to gain control of corporate and company-wide data.

When this situation occurs, it makes sense to develop corporate-level data models which are expanded in detail at the organization or system level. Information engineering provides the means to achieve this. These data models can then be used to interface with structured analysis and design and with structured requirements definition.

12.2.3 Information Engineering and Structured Design

The primary output from structured design is the structure chart, which provides initially a logical module hierarchy at a program or subsystem level, and subsequently a packaged, physical module structure. These logical modules should display minimum coupling and maximum cohesion. Procedure formation produces logical modules which have these attributes. Structure charts could be developed from data flow diagrams using structured analysis and refined by substituting the modules obtained during procedure formation for the lowest-level modules in the charts. Another alternative could be to build structure charts directly from the processes obtained from procedure formation, omitting structured analysis.

12.2.4 HOS, Prototyping, and the Other Techniques

We have already discussed in the chapters on HOS and prototyping that these cannot stand alone. HOS becomes part of the system design and development phases in the ASDM. Prototyping is the rough building or developing of a system to produce the required outputs. Because this rough working model has been produced in a relatively short time period and at minimal cost, it permits iteration of the model until the user is satisfied the system will meet his needs.

12.3 WHITHER THE FUTURE?

This text is about information system specification and design. The approaches it describes are a reflection of the strides made in hardware and software during the last twenty years. The very machine which has been used to type this book, an OSBORNE 1-64K microcomputer, is proof of how far we have come. As microcomputers continue to proliferate with ever-increasing processing power available, the greater the probability that these computers will be linked by communication networks and that office workers will stay at home and work in their own time. This situation will result in more effective use of people's time and vast savings in transportation costs. This also presages a tremendous increase in the number and complexity of computer systems that will be required. Alvin Toffler describes this situation in Chapter 16, "The Electronic Cottage," of his book *The Third Wave* [1].

Designing and building computerized business information systems is not an easy task. It requires the equivalent knowledge and effort that could be required in any major engineering project. Even with the hardware and software available today, a major system using 100,000 lines of COBOL code could take a year or more of elapsed time and several person-years of effort to complete and install. The same system, built using a fourth-generation language such as FOCUS or RAMIS, could probably be put in use in one-fourth of the time with proportionate savings in cost. But even this may not be sufficient in the future. The Japanese are designing a fifth-generation computer which will consist of multiple processors and use a language called PROLOG. This computer is expected to be not only extremely fast, but to be capable of mimicking the human brain.

Even without these powerful computers, giant steps have already been made in the field of artificial intelligence and knowledge-based expert systems. Richard Duda and John Caschnig describe examples of expert systems, including one that is programmed in BASIC for a microcomputer, in a 1981 article called "Knowledge-Based Expert Systems Come of Age" [2].

Artificial intelligence is concerned with making computers perceive, reason, and understand. To do this, computers have to be capable of recognizing "patterns" and "forms" of information rather than facts, just as the human brain does. The problem gets even fuzzier when "hunches" creep into decision making. Among the existing expert systems described by Duda and Caschnig are a medical diagnostic system and a system for aiding prospectors. In every such case, these systems are only as good as the experts who provided the input rules. But the advantage they have is that they can make this knowledge available to every person who has access to the system and has the necessary background to provide the input required.

It would appear, then, that the tools will become available to build complex computerized business systems and to build them fast. What this is not going to eliminate is the need to identify and define the user's requirements, and to convert these requirements into logical information system designs. In other words, the type of material discussed in this book should never become obsolete. What is likely to occur, though, is that better techniques will be discovered to make this logical system design simpler and easier to do. That is the direction that we can expect to follow in the future.

REFERENCES

1. Alvin Toffler, *The Third Wave*, William Morrow & Co., Inc., New York, 1980.
2. Richard Duda and John Caschnig, "Knowledge-Based Expert Systems Come of Age," *BYTE*, September 1981.

Glossary

ASDM Acronym for application system development methodology. *(Chapter 10)*

Action In JSD context, a real-world happening outside the computer system. *(Section 7.2)*

Analyzer A component of HOS USE.IT software. Checks mathematical rules. *(Section 8.8)*

Application Context A term used in structured requirements definition to describe the context in which the application system is to be developed. *(Section 6.4.1)*

Application Functions A term used in structured requirements definition to describe the application system's functions. *(Section 6.4.2)*

Application-Level Entity Diagram Entity diagram drawn at the application system level. *(Section 6.4.1.3)*

Application Results A term used in structured requirements definition to mean the principal outputs from the system. *(Section 6.4.3)*

Assembly Line Diagram A Warnier-Orr diagram that combines the data and the process. *(Section 6.2.3)*

Axes Higher-order software used for describing the functions, data types, and control structures. *(Section 8.8)*

Binary Tree Structure A tree structure in which a parent node can have only two or no children. *(Section 8.3)*

Boundary Clash Occurs when the data input to a process have a different boundary from the data output but are in the same sequence. *(Section 7.3.1)*

Business Data Model Shows the relationships between either business entities or records. At the highest level, a data model reflects entity relationships, while at the lowest level, it reflects a set of normalized records. *(Section 4.3.2)*

Candidate Key A data element in a record which could be used to identify and sequence the record. *(Section 4.4)*

Canonical Schema A schema or user view of data reduced to the simplest and clearest level possible. *(Section 4.3)*

Canonical Synthesis The synthesis of schemas or user views of data to produce a combined canonical schema. *(Section 4.4)*

COBOL A programming language commonly used for business systems. *(Section 3.7)*

Co-Controls In HOS, extensions of primitive structures. *(Section 8.4.2)*

222

Cohesion The act or process of sticking together tightly. In a module, a measure of the elements combining to execute the module's function(s). *(Section 5.3.3)*

CoInclude Co-control structure in HOS. *(Section 8.4.2.3)*

CoJoin Co-control structure in HOS. *(Section 8.4.2.2)*

Combined User-Level Entity Diagram Entity diagram combining several user-level entity diagrams. *(Section 6.4.1.2)*

Concur Co-control structure in HOS. *(Section 8.4.2.1)*

Concurrency Parallelism or multitasking of processes. *(Section 6.2.4)*

Context Diagram The highest level in a data flow diagram, representing the entire system. *(Section 5.2.1.1)*

Control Information Information that provides audit trails. *(Section 1.1)*

CoOr Co-control structure in HOS. *(Section 8.4.2.1)*

Coupling A measure of interdependence between modules. *(Section 5.3.2)*

Cycles/Events In structured requirements definition, refer to the organization of the logical data base. *(Section 6.4.2.4)*

DAD Data-base action diagram. *(Section 4.5.4)*

Data Attribute An elementary item of data that cannot be further subdivided. *Same as* Data Element. *(Section 3.1)*

Data-Base Management System A software package that manages the data stored in a physical data base. *(Section 3.2.1)*

Data Conservation, Principle of A process must be able to build its outputs using only the information in data flows explicitly shown flowing into it, plus constant information (i.e., a process cannot create data by itself, nor can it lose data). *(Section 5.2.1.1)*

Data Element An elementary item of data that cannot be further subdivided. *Same as* Data Attribute. *(Section 3.1)*

Data Flow Diagram A charting tool that traces a network of data flows through a system and provides information at varying levels of detail. *(Section 5.1.1)*

Data Model *See* Business Data Model.

Data Relationship Relationship or association between entities or records in a data model. *(Section 4.3.2)*

Data Stream Connection A stream of sequential messages input to a process. *(Section 7.2.3)*

Data Structure The organization of records in a file or data base. The structure could be logical or physical. *(Section 1.5.1)*

Data Structure Diagram In structured requirements definition, defines the data structure of an output. *(Section 6.2.1)*

Data Use Analysis The analysis of data access paths and record volumes to obtain efficiency in physical data-base design and storage requirements. *(Chapter 11)*

Decision Splitting A type of problem encountered in refining structure charts. A decision is split when recognition and execution affect different entities. *(Section 5.3.4.2)*

Decision Support System A system that provides decision support information. *(Section 1.1)*

Decision Table A table of conditions and actions. *(Section 5.1.1)*

Decision Tree A hierarchical tree of conditions and actions similar to a decision table. *(Section 5.1.1)*

Distribution Analysis Analysis of distributed data and their impact on centralized and decentralized data bases and files. *(Section 4.2)*

Dynamic Model A model that displays a dynamic relationship (e.g., a data flow diagram). *(Section 4.3.2)*

End-User A user who designs and builds his own systems, in particular, systems to query production data bases and files. *(Section 1.2)*

Entity (1) In structured requirements definition, refers to an organizational entity. *(Section 6.4.1)* (2) In Jackson system development, refers to something that exists as part of the real world outside the computer system. It must perform or suffer actions in relation to time. It must be capable of being regarded as an individual or an individual type and of being uniquely named. The system must be required to produce or use information about it. *(Section 7.2)* (3) In information engineering, something that exists in the real world outside the computer system and which is reflected in the data model. It has the same meaning as in Jackson system development. *(Section 4.2)*

Entity Diagram In structured requirements definition, a diagram tracing the flow of outputs between organizational entities. *(Section 6.4.1.1)*

Entity Structure Step Development step in Jackson system development. *(Section 7.2.2)*

Event Function performed during file maintenance and output production. *(Section 4.5)*

External Operation In higher-order software, an operation developed outside HOS. *(Section 8.3)*

Factoring Type of problem encountered in refining structure charts. It is the separation of management-type actions, such as decision making or calling, from work-type actions such as calculating and validating. *(Section 5.3.4.1)*

Fan-In The calling of common modules, in a structure chart, such as error messages and print routines. *(Section 5.3.4.5)*

Fan-Out The number of modules called by a single module in a structure chart. *(Section 5.3.4.3)*

File A repository for stored data. A computer file is a collection of records. *(Section 3.4)*

File Maintenance The processing of input data to update the data stored in a computer file or data base. *(Section 3.4)*

First Normal Form First step in record normalization. Elimination of repeating groups. *(Section 4.3.1.1)*

Flag Condition Condition that identifies when a record is added, deleted, modified, or retrieved. In information engineering, the approach described by Connor to identify procedures. *(Section 4.5.3)*

Flat File A sequential table file with independent records. *(Section 5.2.1)*

Fourth-Generation Language Nonprocedural language in which the instructions define "what is required from the process" rather than "how the process flows." *(Sections 4.2 and 9.1)*

Function (1) In Jackson system development, refers to the production of outputs. *(Section 7.2.4)* (2) Mathematical function where $y = f(x)$. *(Section 8.3)*

Function Step A step in Jackson system development. *(Section 7.2.4)*

Functional Primitive Lowest-level bubble in a data flow diagram. Its content is generally described using structured English, decision tables, or decision trees. *(Section 5.2.1.1)*

HOS Acronym for higher-order software. *(Chapter 8)*

Hierarchy (of records) A family tree of records with any parent record having one or more children records which are dependent on the parent key. *(Section 3.2.1)*

Higher-Order Software Specification and design software, mathematically provable to be correct, developed by Hamilton and Zeldin. *(Chapter 8)*

Implementation Strategy In information engineering, a strategy or activity used to program, test, and implement the system. *(Section 4.2)*

Include Control structure used in HOS. *(Section 8.4.1.2)*

Information Analysis Information engineering strategy or activity used to develop stable data models. *(Section 4.3)*

Information Engineering   Data base–oriented system design and development technique. *(Section 4.1)*

Information System   A system that provides management with human-readable information. *(Section 1.1)*

Interleaving Clash   Occurs when two or more data streams contain the same data. Also referred to as a multithreading clash. *(Section 7.3.3)*

Interval Variable   Data embedded in a computer program which cannot be updated without a program change being made. *(p. 22)*

Iteration   Repetition of the same action in a module or program. *(Section 1.5.2)*

JSD   Acronym for Jackson system development. *(Chapter 7)*

Join   (1) When data elements from two records are combined through a common element to produce a third record. *(Section 4.3.1.4)* (2) Control structure used in HOS. *(Section 8.4.1.1)*

Key   The data element(s) used to identify a record. *(Section 3.1)*

LAM   Acronym for logical access map. Term coined by James Martin to trace the access path through a data model. *(Section 4.5.4)*

Leaf   In a hierarchical tree structure, a child node with no further children. *(Section 8.3)*

Level 1, 2, and 3 Procedures   In information engineering, three levels or stages in procedure formation defined by Clive Finkelstein. *(Section 4.5.2)*

Leveled Diagram   A data flow diagram drawn at different levels, from a context level to a functional primitive. *(Section 5.2.1.1)*

Local Variable   In Jackson system development, the value of an attribute at any point in a program's execution. *(Section 7.2.3)*

Logical Data Base   A data model reflecting logical relationships between records. *(Section 1.5.1)*

Logical Design (of a system)   A system designed in terms of the logical functions to be executed. A logical system must be converted to a physical system before it can be run on a computer. *(Section 1.3)*

Logical Module   A set of computer instructions that execute logical functions. It cannot be stored or accessed. One or more logical modules make up a physical module. *(Section 3.7)*

Logical System   *See* Logical Design.

Mainline Functional Flow   In structured requirements definition, an assembly line diagram linking the principal processes in an application system. *(Section 6.4.2.1)*

Minispecification   Description of the process logic in a functional primitive. *(Section 5.2.1.3)*

Module   A set of computer instructions to execute one or more logical functions. Modules can be logical or physical. *(Section 3.7)*

Multithreading Clash   *See* Interleaving Clash.

Network (of records)   A data base with records linked in pairs. *(Section 3.2.1)*

Node   In a hierarchical tree structure, a parent or child is referred to as a node. *(Section 8.3)*

Normalization   A term coined by E. F. Codd to develop canonical data structures. *(Section 4.3)*

Normalized Record   An independent and stable record developed through the normalization process. *(Section 4.3.1)*

Objectives   In structured requirements definition, used to define the application system's functions. *(Section 6.4.1.3)*

Operating Information   Information required to maintain a business's operations (e.g., daily production counts, checks paid, and invoice information). *(Section 1.1)*

Operating System   The software that controls the execution of computer programs. *(Section 3.7)*

Operational Objective   An objective defined at the operational level (i.e., the worker or producer level). For example, "To produce 1000 widgets per week with fewer than 1 percent defective." *(Section 4.2)*

Or   Control structure in HOS. *(Section 8.4.1.3)*

Ordering Clash   Occurs when the data input to a process is in a different sequence to the data output. *(Section 7.3.3)*

Output Oriented   System specification and design based on human-readable outputs. *(Chapter 6)*

Packaging   The combining of logical module processes to provide physical modules or programs. *(Section 5.3.8)*

Physical Data Base   A data base or file in which data are stored. *(Sections 1.5.1 and 4.2)*

Physical File   The actual working file. See Physical Data Base.

Physical Module   A set of computer instructions consisting of one or more logical modules. It can be stored in a library and can be called by a program or another physical module when it is to be executed. *(Section 3.7)*

Physical System   A computer system that can be executed on a computer. *(Section 3.7)*

Primitive   In HOS, refers to a primitive control structure. *(Section 8.4.1)*

Primitive Bubble   *See* Functional Primitive.

Primitive Construct   *See* Primitive.

Primitive Control Structure   *See* Primitive.

Primitive Operation   In HOS, an operation that cannot be broken down further. *(Section 8.3)*

Procedure   A series of steps to be followed to complete a process. *(Section 1.5.1)*

Procedure Formation   In information engineering, those strategies or activities used to develop manual and computer procedures. *(Section 4.2)*

Process   A continuous operation to achieve an end. *(Section 1.5.1)*

Process-Driven System   A system design based on a series of related processes. *(Section 1.3)*

Program   A named physical entity in a computer system which can stand alone, can be stored in a library, and has a fixed physical organization. It generally consists of one or more physical modules. *(Section 3.7)*

Program Specification Synthesis   In information engineering, a technique used to produce program code from predefined, common modules stored in a data dictionary. *(Section 4.2)*

Projection   When certain data elements from one record are reorganized to produce a second. *(Section 4.3.1.4)*

Prototype   "An original or model on which something is patterned or a first full-scale and usually functional form of a new type or design of a construction (as an airplane)" *(Webster's New Collegiate Dictionary). (Section 9.1)*

RAT   Resource Allocation Tool. Component of HOS USE.IT software. Uses the output from ANALYZER and generates executable program code. *(Section 8.8)*

Record   A named set of data elements identified by one or more keys. *(Section 3.2)*

Recursive Operation   A loop or recursion executed during iteration in a program or module. *(Section 8.3)*

Relation Set   A set of records linked by relational algebra or calculus stored in a database management system. *(Section 3.2.1)*

Repeating Group   A group of data elements in a record which occurs more than once per record. *(Section 4.3.1.1)*

Root   The topmost node in a hierarchical data structure. *(Section 8.3)*

Root Key   The key of the root segment (topmost segment, which is not dependent on any other segment) in a canonical data model. *(Section 4.4)*

Schema   A diagrammatic representation of records (segments) and their associations or relationships. *(Section 4.3)*

Second Normal Form   Second stage in record normalization where every data element in the record is made dependent on every data element in the primary key. *(Section 4.3.1.2)*

Secondary Record   A record that can be derived from the data elements in the canonical data model but which is consistently required. These records, if stored, reduce processing time. *(Section 4.6.2)*

Segment   A term used to describe a group of data elements which are linked together to form a whole. It is the basic group of data passed to and from a program under the control of data-base software. Each record in a canonical data model is a segment. *(Section 4.4)*

Selection   Selection of an action in a module or program. *(Section 1.5.2)*

Sequence   A series of consecutive actions in a module or program. *(Section 1.5.2)*

Set of Relations (of records)   *See* Relation Set.

Standard Module   A module developed in line with a standard function which can be used or called as needed by other modules or programs. *(Section 4.6.4)*

State Vector   In Jackson system development, the set of all the local variables in a particular process. *(Section 7.2.3)*

State-Vector Connection   In Jackson system development, occurs when one process inspects the state vector of another process. *(Section 7.2.3)*

Static Model   A model that displays static relationships (e.g., a data model). *(Section 4.3.2)*

Stepwise Refinement   A design technique in which information is recorded in a hierarchy where a parent is expanded into several children which, in turn, become parents of other children. An example is a leveled data flow diagram. *(Section 1.3)*

Strategic Objective   An organization objective defined to satisfy the organization's mission and purpose. Strategic objectives generally extend over three- to five-year time periods. *(Section 4.2)*

Strategic Requirements Planning   The group of techniques associated with planning requirements for long-range strategies. *(Section 4.2)*

Structure Chart   A hierarchy of modules that call one another and pass data and control between them. *(Section 5.3.1)*

Structure Clash   Refers to a data structure clash between the structures of an input and an output. *(Sections 6.7 and 7.3)*

Structure Diagram   In Jackson system development, an abstract model of the real world. *(Section 7.2.2)*

Structure Text   In Jackson system development, the notation used to describe a process. *(Section 7.2.3)*

Structured   A system design or a process having a specific organization structure. *(Section 1.3)*

Structured English   A basic form of English using the three basic programming constructs (i.e., sequence, selection, and iteration). *(Section 5.2.1.3)*

System   A set of processes to meet specific needs. These needs are met by specific outputs. To provide these outputs, data are input and stored. *(Section 3.7)*

System Implementation Diagram   In Jackson system development, the diagram used to display the relationship between the files, processes, inputs, and outputs in the system. *(Section 7.2.6)*

System Implementation Step   A step in Jackson system development. *(Section 7.2.6)*

System Specification Diagram   In Jackson system development, used to represent the connection between the real world and the model. *(Section 7.2.3)*

Systems Maintenance   Correction of problems in a production system. Can also include enhancements or modifications to the original design. *(Section 1.1)*

System Timing Step   A step in Jackson system development. *(Section 7.2.5)*

Tactical Objective An objective defined at a higher level than an operational objective, generally on an annual basis and involving detailed planning with a specific budget. *(Section 4.2)*

Text Pointer In Jackson system development, the special variable in a process which indicates where the last instruction was executed in a program. *(Section 7.2.3)*

Third Normal Form Third stage in the record normalization process, in which data elements dependent on other nonprimary key data elements result in further record expansion. *(Section 4.3.1.3)*

Transaction In structured requirements definition, refers to the organization of the logical data base in terms of transactions. *(Section 6.4.2.4)*

Transaction Analysis In structured analysis and design, the development of structure charts based on transactions. *(Section 5.3.6)*

Transform Analysis In structured analysis and design, the development of structure charts based on sequential processes. *(Section 5.3.5)*

USE.IT Software Higher-order software consisting of three components (i.e., AXES, ANALYZER, and RAT). *(Section 8.8)*

User-Level Entity Diagram Entity diagram drawn at the user level. *(Section 6.4.1.1)*

Userview A set of records or segments required by an output such as a report or another system/subsystem. Also referred to as a schema. *See* Schema. *(Section 4.3)*

Warnier-Orr Diagram Analysis and design tool that uses brackets to display hierarchical systems and data structures. *(Section 6.2)*

Zero-Level Diagram In a data flow diagram, the expansion of the context diagram to include the major processes. *(Section 5.2.1.1)*

Index